1970

TEACHING
AMERICAN PRONUNCIATION
TO
FOREIGN STUDENTS

TEACHING
AMERICAN PRONUNCIATION
TO
FOREIGN STUDENTS

By

MITCHELL R. BURKOWSKY, Ph.D.

Division of Special Education and Rehabilitation
Syracuse University
Syracuse, New York

WARREN H. GREEN, INC.
St. Louis, Missouri, U.S.A.

Published and distributed by

WARREN H. GREEN, INC.
10 South Brentwood Blvd.
St. Louis, Missouri 63105, U.S.A.

Printed in the United States of America
4-A

ACKNOWLEDGMENTS

A MONG THE MANY individuals who knowingly or unknowingly influenced this book are several former professors and/or colleagues listed below in alphabetical order and identified in terms of their locations at the time that I experienced their influence:

Dr. Paul Boomsliter, State University of New York at Albany
Dr. Kenneth Bzoch, University of Florida
Dr. Donald Dew, University of Florida
Dr. John Duffy, Brooklyn College
Dr. George Kopp, Wayne State University
Dr. Pierre Léon, Phonetic Institute of France
Dr. Donald Lloyd, Wayne State University
Dr. Edgar Mayer, Wayne State University
Dr. Robert West, Brooklyn College

Much of the methodological approach presented here resulted from two years of close association with Professor Mayer and the English for Foreign Students Program at Wayne State University. Several insights with reference to the socialization problems of foreign students ensued from discussions with Dr. Richard Bedford of Wayne State University and with Dr. Mayer.

Miss Maureen Moran supplied Appendices B and C which were outgrowths of a directed study done under my supervision at Syracuse University. An experienced speech therapist, she combined speech therapy and language techniques with an outgoing personality in such a manner that her students responded positively not only in attitude, but in progress toward acquisition of better comprehension and use of American English.

Mrs. Terry Morrison has patiently and competently assisted me in typing the various drafts so that copies could be provided for my students to "field-test" at the Syracuse University Speech Clinic. She has caught many of my minor and major errors.

Miss Patricia Downs made valuable suggestions for the book cover designs. Mr. John Genauer and Mrs. Elizabeth DeBoer generously assisted in the preparation of the indexes.

To the publisher of the *Minneapolis Star* I offer thanks for permission to quote *Language Lesson* by Harriet Voxland.

MITCHELL R. BURKOWSKY
Syracuse, New York

CONTENTS

                                                              Page
Acknowledgments   v
Chapter
   I.   To the Unsophisticated Teacher or Therapist   3
  II.   Basic Concepts of Teaching CAE Pronunciation   5
 III.   Choosing Appropriate Pedagogical Media   11
  IV.   Auditory Training   17
   V.   Visual Training   22
  VI.   Kinesthetic-Proprioceptive Training   26
 VII.   Use of Context   30
VIII.   Personalizing the Subject Matter   34
  IX.   Supplementary Sources of Ideas and Drill Material   38
   X.   Sample Procedures   44
  XI.   Phonetics as a Tool   49
 XII.   Individual Therapy   55
XIII.   Group Therapy   77

Epilogue: Termination of Training 101
Selected References 103
Appendix A: Speech Texts to be Used as Sources 107
Appendix B: Summary of a Group Program by Maureen Moran 111
Appendix C: Moran Survey of English Usage by Maureen Moran 115
Indices 123

TEACHING
AMERICAN PRONUNCIATION
TO
FOREIGN STUDENTS

CHAPTER I

TO THE UNSOPHISTICATED TEACHER OR THERAPIST

T his text is not intended for the highly trained and sophisticated linguist, nor for the speech pathologist who has had a considerable amount of theory and practicum with foreign students. It is directed toward educators who suddenly find themselves with students who have oral communication problems primarily because their native language is not American English. It is also aimed at the student speech pathologist or therapist who has been told: "Here's a foreign accent case for you; go to work!"

Any relatively good native speaker of colloquial American English (hereafter to be written CAE) should be able to work at the application of a few basic rules in such a way that his student should: 1) learn to understand native speakers better; 2) develop more confidence in his own ability to communicate orally in CAE, and 3) be better understood by the natives. If the teacher has some background in phonetics, oral interpretation or languages, the basic concepts in the following chapter should be familiar. If he doesn't have the advantage of such course work, it may take a little longer, but not too much longer, to understand them. The basic concepts are so deceptively simple that too much sophistication in formal English usage may hinder their comprehension. Formal English was originally established according to rules intended for classical Latin and Greek. Modern English, which has borrowed extensively from several languages and language systems, does not resemble the classical languages from which formal English was codified. Currently, there is a movement in the fields of English and language to teach the language as it is spoken by the relatively cultured native speakers rather than according to artificial classical rules.

In this book, the emphasis will definitely follow the "modern" approach, with stress upon teaching the foreign student to ad-

3

just to the surprisingly sloppy speech of classroom instructors, fellow students, and people with whom he will come into daily contact. Many foreign students have told me that their realization of this standard sloppiness helped them more than any other concept in the comprehension of spoken English. In Chapter II are presented some relatively universal generalizations which may be made concerning the reasons for CAE pronunciation being normally indistinct (Judson and Weaver, 1965; MacDonald, 1964).

Centers which train linguists have sought basic dynamic approaches to teaching written and oral language and have discovered that the blending of one sound into another and words into phrases is quite common in several languages, French being but one example. The lack of alphabetical symbols to correspond with actual pronunciation has been another stumbling block in the teaching of most languages. In efforts to overcome this problem, new and exciting approaches to the understanding and teaching of phonetic concepts have led to the scrapping of rigid phonetic systems in favor of eclectic and experimental approaches wherein missionaries, for example, develop phonetic alphabets in terms of the needs of the language for which they are compiling dictionaries and grammars. Each language is scrutinized as much as possible according to its dynamic communicative bases. American English is beginning to be viewed in this new orientation toward communication. It is my hope that this book reflects this orientation.

CHAPTER II

BASIC CONCEPTS OF TEACHING CAE PRONUNCIATION

1. *American English is not pronounced as it is spelled.* Look carefully at the above sentence. The letter *a* at the beginning of the first word is not usually pronounced like any other *a* in the sentence. It would most probably approximate the sound that is often written as *uh*. The second *a* is customarily quite short, almost swallowed, and varies in pronunciation from speaker to speaker and from one repetition to another by the same speaker. The *a* in *as* has a variety of normal pronunciations depending on how the sentence is broken into phrases. *E* in *American* may resemble the first *e* of *spelled* in pronunciation, but the *e* in *English* more closely resembles the sound of *i* as in *it*, while the *e*'s in *pronounced* and *spelled* (second *e*) are silent.

Now, try to write the same sentence as you would say it! You will notice that in some cases two letters together comprise one sound, as with *ng* and *sh* in *English*—seven letters for five sounds. The *d* of *pronounced* sounds like *t*, but the same letter in *spelled* equals a slightly muffled *d*. None of the *o*'s are pronounced similarly.

Listen carefully to other native speakers while they say the sentence. How many acceptable variations in pronunciation do you notice for this sentence alone? Do members of your own family necessarily pronounce the sentence as you do? Do the separate words of the sentence have different pronunciations when spoken in isolation? This leads to the second basic concept.

2. *English is not pronounced as it is spaced on paper.* In the above sentence there are ten words which in CAE would be pronounced as one long word. The last part of one word may often be slurred into the next so that all the words within an average phrase may be hard to distinguish from one another. This concept is known as *liaison* or *linking* and exists in many modern languages. *Liaison* is normal. Breaking the phrase into separate words

5

is abnormal and was developed primarily as an aid to visual understanding of the printed or written page. Let's remove the spaces between the words of Rule 2:

Englishisnotpronouncedasitisspacedonpaper.

Confusing, isn't it? Yet this is a more legitimate manner of writing it according to the phrasing. Unfortunately, the artificial visual crutch of word separation is standardly employed as the pedagogical basis for pronunciation. Teachers of children and adolescents spend a great deal of time having students memorize the arbitrary spellings of these isolated units of communication, but rarely teach the reasons why these words are pronounced differently in connected speech than they are in isolation. In isolation, each word is stressed. In connected speech, the important words are stressed and the unimportant words are minimized, sometimes to the point of becoming lost. For example: *What are you doing?* may deteriorate to *What're you doing?*, or *Whatcha doin?* Pity the poor foreign student who tries to look up *Whatcha* (or more likely *wutshuh*) in a dictionary! The typical foreign student has learned the combinations of letters that equal specific sounds in his native language. If that language employs the same written symbols as English they are apt to be pronounced quite differently in several instances. Thus, due to ignorance of Rules 1 and 2, the naive foreign student is at a disadvantage when *listening* to words which he is capable of *reading* quite well.

Ignorance of Rule 2 also leads to a plodding word-by-word speech pattern, with each word receiving almost equal stress. This lends a monotonous, strained quality to the speech. Many natives become impatient and uncomfortable when listening to such a pattern, especially those who have never been in a similar situation, and a breakdown in communications may result fairly soon if the listener becomes bored. Rule 3 overlaps with rules 1 and 2.

3. *The vowels of CAE are usually quite different than the vowels of other languages.* Phonetics texts often state that there are sixteen or seventeen vowels in American English, depending on the dialect spoken. Yet, when the foreign student listens carefully, he quite often perceives what *we* consider vowels to be

diphthongs according to the language system in which he was raised. Many American students of French have been told that they and the British chew French vowels like a cow. In a sense this is true, for we generally move our tongues and jaws more lazily and less precisely when speaking than do speakers of most of the other major languages in the world. This lack of deliberateness in speech production commonly results in a speaker's inability to say a short phrase three times in a row with the same pronunciation, yet he is understood quite easily by other Americans. Why? The native American is accustomed to doing the same thing. He attends to the important word in the phrase, having learned to disregard unimportant connective words and their telescoped pronunciations, most of which telescoping affects the vowels to a greater extent than it does the consonants. In CAE, then, two confusingly opposite things happen to vowels:

1) They become prolonged, diphthongized and distorted, and

2) They become shortened, distorted, or disappear.

The vowel varies in pronunciation according to its relative importance within the spoken phrase. It is the vowel that most often carries the emotion, the intensity, the pitch change and the timing of the phrase. Alteration of the vowel's pronunciations within a phrase may well alter the meaning of the phrase. Read the following sentences aloud conversationally according to the indicated emphases:

1. *I* can do that.
2. I *can* do that.
3. I can *do* that.
4. I can do *that*.

The good speaker of CAE should "swallow" or shorten the vowel in *can* in examples 1, 3, and 4 as the vowels in the stressed words increase in prominence. An exercise with a similar intent often employed by teachers of oral interpretation or voice and diction is to have the student say the word *no* seven different ways to connote seven different meanings.

4. *When an American sound does not exist in the foreign student's native language, he will substitute for it the most similar sound or sounds of his own language.* He may not be fully

aware that he is doing so even after having been informed of his error. The sound represented by *a* in *cat* is among the most difficult for speakers of Greek, Spanish, and Slavic languages. Their usual substitution is similar to the vowel in *pop*. Another problem sound is the vowel in *him*. Many foreign students substitute a sound which is just a shade off that pronunciation, tending toward but not approximating the vowel sound in *he*. This substituted sound may be employed for either *he* or *him*. The two *th* sounds as in *the* and *thin* are commonly mispronounced by the vast majority of foreign students unless they have learned the correct pronunciations relatively early in life. Substitutions for the *th*'s may include *d, t, z,* and *s*. In some cultures, it is considered impolite to protrude the tongue, which makes it somewhat difficult to employ tongue protrusion as a technique for teaching *th*. American *r*'s standardly present problems because they are more vowel-like than in most languages. There is no stoppage of the exhaled breath stream in our *r*'s, whereas in other languages the back or tip of the tongue or the soft palate may interrupt the airflow one or more times in *r* production.

5. *It is more important to teach the overall pattern of phrases than it is to teach specific sounds.* The rhythm of a language is basic to its accurate comprehension. We have all experienced situations wherein someone has shouted to us from a distance so that the sounds are muffled but the message is still perceived on the basis of the stress pattern. In teaching deaf or hard-of-hearing children to speak, early training in rhythm and phrase patterning leads to more normal speech than do approaches of a more segmental nature. Adding specific sound productions to the phrasal patterns is quite normal in a child's linguistic maturation since the vowels and vowel-like elements which comprise the stress pattern customarily develop earlier in children than do the consonants. As the child becomes more aware of his sound-producing ability and of the fine differentiations in the speech of others, he tends to monitor himself in such a way as to refine and delicately adjust his speech mechanism for the more precise production of consonants. Why not employ this concept with the foreign student?

6. *When a student demands rules for given phrases or pronunciations and you don't know any, admit it.* This is not an unusual situation. CAE is burdened with and enlivened by numerous words, phrases and expressions which make no sense when analyzed logically. These may or may not be colloquial expressions, idioms or jargon specific to an occupation or profession. These may be taught in a memorized fashion with their intent explained any way you can. It is best to present a context in which the meaning is easily deduced. The more one works with foreign students the more it becomes apparent that pronunciation, meaning and culture often must be taught at the same time, in a combined inductive-deductive fashion.

7. *When a student cannot learn pronunciation through one sensory modality, try other sensory approaches.* Although careful listening may help some students to learn correct pronunciation, others may learn better by looking at the movements of the teacher's face. Still others need to have their speech articulators physically manipulated by the instructor so that they may feel the difference in direction and extent of movement of their articulators (tongue, jaw, lips, palate, teeth). Various combinations work better with one student than with another. A tape recorder may be all that one student needs, while another may need to look at himself in a mirror while imitating the teacher. Electronic motivating machines may help a third, but, alas! nothing may help a fourth. As in all educational fields, there is the ever-present problem of individual variation.

8. *The younger the student—all other variables being equal— the better the chance for success.* Among the most difficult to teach CAE are those who have been in this country for a long time during which they spoke English incorrectly. It is easier to teach CAE "from scratch" than it is to change well-habituated incorrect speech production. Children as old as fifteen or sixteen appear to be more adaptable to new learning patterns than do their elders, but even some teen-agers have become relatively rigid in intellectual and behavioral patterns at earlier ages than one would anticipate.

9. *Use any approach that works!* No two people are the same.

That includes teachers. What may work for one may not be effective for another. One person may feel comfortable working in a highly structured fashion while another may perform better in a more flexible orientation. Whatever approach the teacher uses should be one in which he does not perceive himself as behaving artificially, for artificiality may impede the communication that is the goal of the learning situation.

CHAPTER III

CHOOSING APPROPRIATE PEDAGOGICAL MEDIA

A. THE TOOLS

A WELL-EQUIPPED CENTER for teaching second languages should have a variety of visual, auditory, and audio-visual devices to be used as aids to instruction. Among the most commonly-employed aids are recordings. The disc or tape recording to accompany a written text has been used relatively successfully in the teaching of several languages. In this approach, the following variations may be employed:

1) The student may first read the version in his own language silently, read the second language version silently, and then listen to the second language with or without looking at the written version;

2) The student may first listen to the second language recording while looking at the written version, try to understand with no supplementary aid, and then either read or play his native language version, after which he replays the second language recording;

3) A contextual orientation may be given to the student before he listens to the second-language recording so that he may mentally conjure appropriate sequences into which the foreign phrases should logically fall;

4) A teaching machine may be employed with the recorder in such a way that questions may be asked and a series of alternate written or oral answers provided so that the student may correct himself;

5) A written text may be projected upon a screen while a recording by a native speaker of the second language is played so that the student may first listen and then read aloud in time with the recording. There are several other variations upon this theme, especially since the development of relatively inexpensive

11

tape recorders which lend versatility to audio-visual approaches. Tapes are rapidly replacing discs in language teaching.

A relatively recent training tool is the improved version of the Bell and Howell Language Master. This is a modified tape recorder which is activated by inserting a card between the playback heads. On the card is a strip of magnetic tape plus a word, sentence, picture, or combination thereof. It is also possible for the instructor to record new practice material on these or other cards so that the student may work with the machine on his own. The Language Master has proven to be quite helpful in a variety of learning situations.

Short sound films with simple plots may be used in conjunction with vocabulary and grammar lessons. These may be so constructed that they become increasingly difficult and complex as the student progresses. Such films may be shown over and over until the student is capable of predicting the phrasing.

The typical language laboratory emphasizes an auditory orientation. Usually, the student requests the laboratory assistant to play a specific recording so that he (in an enclosed booth) may listen, repeat while recording on another tape, and play back both tapes in order to compare and self-correct errors. This technique is most effective when immediately monitored by an expert speaker of the second language. Unfortunately, budgets for most language laboratories rarely extend far enough to pay for qualified human monitors.

Slide projectors, overhead projectors, opaque projectors and film strip projectors may be employed to present a variety of visual images for discussion and/or drill. These may be synchronized with recorded material so that an instructor need not be present while the student rehearses.

Among primarily visual aids, one may find pictures to discuss, charts with lists of phrases, other charts with rules, cartoons to demonstrate points, boards with facial contours painted upon them with flexible bicycle chains attached in such a manner that they may be used to demonstrate how the speech articulators move in the production of certain sounds, picture stories to follow, and three dimensional objects.

The above and many other ingenious and expensive devices are useful in second language teaching. For practical purposes, and for most of the readers for whom this book is intended, very few of these pedagogical media will be of much use unless such equipment and space are available, and unless the equipment is in good working condition. From bitter experience with audio-visual equipment, it is my opinion that it is dangerous to plan a great deal of instruction around machinery for the following reasons: 1) machinery quite often breaks down or does not arrive when the whole lesson for the day is based upon that specific piece of equipment; 2) certain devices require rooms with acoustic qualities or sizes not readily available—and it is surprising how few electrical outlets there are in some school buildings; 3) preparation of audio-visual material is a time-consuming task; 4) purchasing materials for daily lessons necessitates budget planning and ordering far in advance; 5) over-reliance on audio-visual techniques limits the flexibility of the teacher or therapist; 6) when you get right down to it the best audio-visual aid is the instructor, who may be seen and heard by the student.

Minimal instructional media for our purposes are: 1) the instructor; 2) some means of graphic representation, such as a chalkboard and chalk, or paper and pencil, pen, crayon, felt marker, etc.; 3) a tape recorder or equivalent; 4) a mirror large enough so that the faces of the student and the teacher may both be seen at the same time.

Supplementary aids may include other students or native speakers, books, magazines, radio and television. Mail-order catalogs are rich sources of discussion material. Periodicals similar to *Readers Digest* contain short, colloquial items laden with humor and idioms—two of the most difficult things to learn in a foreign language, since humor is often couched in idiomatic terms which have little meaning when translated literally.

B. THE DYNAMICS

In a typical educational institution, space is nearly always a problem. Ideally, instruction should be carried on in a relatively quiet, well-illuminated and well-ventilated room with sufficient wall space and electrical outlets to enable the instructor to utilize audio-visual techniques. I was once assigned such a room in which the windows did not open because the entire building was air conditioned. All during that summer the air conditioning did not work in that room. Neither I as a teacher nor my students performed well in that room. We elected to move to a building where we could breathe better but not use as many audio-visual devices. We were fortunate to have a choice of rooms. Many teachers are not that fortunate. At times, room availability is so restricted that instruction may be conducted in a hallway, under stairs, in teachers' lounges, in boiler rooms, in closets, and in waiting rooms. It is surprising how much effective work may be accomplished in such conditions.

The pedagogical devices and space needed are to a great measure dependent upon the number of students to be seen at one time. If there is but one student, it is fairly easy to plan space and lessons, but if there are two or more students—even from the same country—it becomes necessary to think in terms of their having individual as well as group training. How many foreign students may be grouped successfully at one time? Do the students' native languages determine how the grouping is to be done? Are age and number of years in this country to be used as criteria for grouping? Should the teacher approach grouping in terms of levels or should all be subjected to the same material? Let us discuss these questions.

Grouping the Students. If students are on noticeably different levels with regard to English ability, it is usually better to group them accordingly for presentation of theory, but an experienced teacher will often combine them in a fashion similar to that employed by a teacher of a one-room school house, working with the various levels in turn during the session. It is convenient to think in terms of group discussion concepts rather than general educational concepts in determining the size of the group. Five to eight students should be considered a good-sized class. More than this number makes it difficult for the teacher to alternate group drill with individual drill so that a student's grasp of a concept or pronunciation may be determined.

If all of the students to be grouped are from one country, there may be a caste system to contend with, for despite advances in science, industry and politics, there are still some countries whose populace look askance at one another according to religion, income, color and educational or professional background. The teacher should be aware of these possible conflicts and handle them according to his own capabilities. Nationalism may be another problem; Israeli *sabras* and ex-Israeli arabs in the same class may lead to conflict rather than cooperation. Another aspect of nationalism may be noted in the following example: in the late 1950's, after the Hungarian revolts, several young Hungarian adults who escaped the country arrived in the United States. They were here only reluctantly at first and had, on the whole, little desire of becoming American citizens. Their purpose for learning English was primarily so that they could earn enough money to be able to return to Hungary. At that time, I had several Hungarian students whose interests were such that they insisted on carrying on conversations with each other in Hungarian during classes regardless of who was speaking. They would sit next to one another in class and resist attempts to have them seated next to non-Hungarians. One Hungarian with whom I am working presently is a graduate engineer. This is his eighth year in the country and he has just begun to study English at the demand of his employer who told him to either learn English or be fired.

The student who has been in an English-speaking country long enough to acquire basic vocabulary for activities of daily life should perhaps be grouped apart from the new arrival who lacks basic terminology. Strangely enough, the recently arrived student may pick up appropriate language patterns more quickly and thoroughly than his compatriot who has been in the country for awhile without formally studying the language for the following reasons: 1) with good teaching methods, he should learn basic terminology and patterns of speech before he has an opportunity to ingrain poor speech habits; 2) if he begins to study English immediately upon arriving in this country, he will spend less time floundering around insecurely in conversations for his attitude will often be more questioning and open; 3) he is more likely to admit that he doesn't understand something than will his countryman who has lived here longer. Sometimes grouping the two together may render the "older" student less secure when he compares their relative progress.

If several nationalities are represented in your students, you may decide to group them according to similar characteristics of their native languages so that, for example, South Americans whose native languages are dialects of Spanish and Portuguese may be grouped with European speakers of romance languages. Speakers of tonemic languages like Chinese dialects and Thai may be grouped together quite effectively. Yet, conversely, sometimes the grouping of students from quite different language areas may be used advantageously to teach the students fine discriminations between almost similar sounds in the various languages as well as the facial and lingual movements appropriate to their production.

Whatever the grouping, time should be alotted for individual training for each student. Attempts should be made to place him in exclusively English-speaking environments as much as possible. He should be encouraged to ask questions and to let people know that he does not understand them.

CHAPTER IV

AUDITORY TRAINING

BLACK *et al.* (1965) studied listening and speaking abilities of 24 Spanish-, 24 Japanese-, and 24 Hindi-speaking individuals for whom English was a second language. They found that "the groups that had been established on the basis of listening were different in their speech. The better listeners were the more intelligible speakers; the better listeners were rated as having less foreignism in their speech; and the better listeners spent a greater amount of time vocalizing" (p.48). The results of this study should not be surprising to many language teachers trained after World War II, for it was during that war and the subsequent Asiatic conflicts the "total immersion" concepts of teaching language became widely used and promulgated. Military installations such as the language-training school at Monterey and private institutions (of which Middlebury College is an example) insisted that their students read, write and converse exclusively in the language that they were learning during their entire daily schedule. It was felt that the student should thus be conditioned holistically through all of his learning media.

How does such an approach work? If a student is hungry and cannot eat until he learns to ask for food properly, he will soon pay careful attention to the speech of those who know how to ask for food. If he has difficulty following directions and gets penalized accordingly, he soon learns to pay close attention to directions. In sum, it is a *focussing of attention* that becomes important in learning situations. Auditory training is merely one means of attempting to teach a student to focus upon stimuli. Other avenues for focussing include sight, smell, taste and touch. Later chapters will discuss visual training and kinesthetic-proprioceptive training. Smell and taste will not be treated extensively here, but they may be quite effectively used in second-language teaching in conjunction with visual stimuli. For example, the teacher may

17

pretend to smell an item, make appreciative facial and gestural motions, and then say "that smells wonderful!"

Some people have better auditory than visual memories while with others the converse may be true. Many may learn better by physically repeating patterns in order to feel the muscular and joint-movement patterns. Your students will soon demonstrate their weak modalities.

During the first session, it is advisable to assess the student's ability to: (1) hear, and (2) understand what he apparently hears. If there is a hearing deficiency remediable through medication, surgery or hearing aids, appropriate steps should be taken to ensure that the hearing problem be taken care of as soon as possible. Difficulty in understanding may result from neurological damage, lack of vocabulary or insufficient motivation. Mental retardation, physical fatigue and generally poor psychophysical condition should be considered as possibilities to be ruled out.

Assuming that your student has normal hearing and is free from aberrant physical and psychological problems, one may begin with auditory discrimination testing which often turns out to be a training process at the same time. Dr. Edgar Mayer, formerly of Wayne State University, had drawings made for testing and teaching purposes which demonstrated minimal pairs. In the concept of *minimal pairs,* two words are selected so that they differ from one another by only one sound. An example would be *ship* as compared with *sheep,* where only the vowel made the difference in meaning. Another pair would be *sheep* and *cheap.*

You may have noticed that it is easier to draw *sheep* and *ship* than to draw the concept of *cheap.* This leads to two major approaches of testing the student's auditory discrimination. In the first approach, several pictures with minimal pair items may be presented to the student while the teacher or a recording pronounces the words for the student to identify. The teacher notes correct and incorrect responses. In the second approach a series of sentences may be spoken by the instructor or presented via recordings while the student indicates on an answer sheet which of two or more sentences he has heard. Some examples are:

1. A. I'm going to buy a house.

   B. I'm going to buy a mouse.

2. A. When is she going to school?

   B. When is he going to school?

3. A. May I borrow your soup?

   B. May I borrow your soap?

4. A. He slept on a small cat.

   B. He slept on a small cot.

5. A. She slept a lot.

   B. She slipped a lot.

6. A. Her name is Ruth.

   B. Her name is Root.

The responses may then be tabulated and categorized so that the teacher may ascertain those sounds with which his student has the most difficulty. Ideally, minimal pair tests should include a sufficient variety of sound combinations so that most of the sounds in the language are represented. To test all sound combinations in CAE is time-consuming and not really necessary. The student's speech will soon direct your attention to those phonemes (sounds) with which he has the most difficulty. Be sure, however to test the vowels thoroughly, for, as was mentioned above, vowel and diphthong usage is of more than ordinary significance to foreign students. Certain consonants invariably present problems: r, l, th, sh, ch, w, v, ng, and the first sound in the word *jump*. At least these consonants should be tested.

A more complicated means of evaluating auditory discrimination is to dictate several words or sentences while the student writes what he thinks you are saying. This tests not only discrimination, but also comprehension and writing skills, and as such, may give you too much information at one time.

Since much meaning in many languages is conveyed by differences in pitch, relative loudness, and length of sounds, it is feasible to determine just how aware the student is of these dimensions. After his attention is focussed on these characteristics, they may be employed as pedagogical concepts.

Pitch discrimination may be tested and taught in a variety of manners. The teacher may whistle or play two different tones for the student to differentiate. He may have two or more students say a sound or word and have the other students indicate the speaker with the higher or lower voice. He may stamp on the floor with his foot and then hiss, again requesting a discrimination with reference to highness or lowness of pitch. A more sophisticated phonographic test battery of pitch and other discriminations was developed at the University of Iowa (The Seashore Tests) and is often found in the libraries of Music, Psychology, Physics and Speech departments of colleges and universities. This test has multiple uses and has been employed to predetermine relative success of students in phonetics courses in college as well as to select individuals to train in other skills.

Relative loudness is important in the stress patterns of CAE, since a lack of loudness differentiation reduces the meaningfulness and vitality of a phrase. Quite often, foreign students will maintain one loudness level throughout their utterances as part of their previous training in reading English. Perhaps it is best to test for loudness concepts only perfunctorily and then immediately concentrate on the importance of loudness in speech context. Teach loudness as only one means of producing stress and contrast in CAE. Show how loudness, pitch variation, pause and prolongation serve separately and in combination to produce the melodic patterns of the language. This may be done by playing a short tape recording of conversational speech several times for each of the concepts you wish to demonstrate. Thus, the first time through the student may listen for meaning. The second time you tell him to look for pitch variation. After you tell him what he should have heard with reference to pitch, play the recording as many times as necessary for him and for you to be certain that he can duplicate the pitch pattern orally. With the same recording, you may then follow similar procedures with loudness, pause, prolongation and specific phonemic difficulties. Analyzing one short sentence in this agonizing manner may be of more ultimate benefit than doing a variety of other exercises.

When the student practices duplicating the pronunciation of the practice phrase, his efforts should be tape-recorded so that he may obtain sufficient auditory feedback to monitor his next verbal output. The instructor's comments should be tape recorded at the same time so that student may have an opportunity to re-evaluate what he said in relation to the instructor's critique.

A series of follow-up assignments based on this would consist of having the student listen to good and bad CAE speakers, evaluating their use of the specific aspects recently studied. Having the foreign students in the group evaluate one another in a similar fashion often stimulates a friendly rivalry which enhances the learning.

CHAPTER V

VISUAL TRAINING

L IP READING HAS long been considered a compensatory means
to be employed by the deaf and hard of hearing for: a) better
comprehension, and b) visible aid in the learning of new coordinations for the production of sounds. In conventional speech
therapy, the student is often encouraged to imitate the physical
movements of his therapist's speech articulators—lips, teeth, jaws,
soft palate and tongue. Sophisticated teachers of English to speakers of other languages are aware of the visual aspects of speech
and wisely utilize visual training to supplement other standard
techniques. The more a teacher works with people who have
varied speech disorders the more he discovers that techniques
usually affiliated with the remediation of one problem work
equally well, if not better, with types of problems with which
one would not usually associate such techniques.

The human face is capable of myriad combinations of movements which may express as many shades of emotion or opinion.
These facial movements may inform the listener-watcher that the
words being said are only in jest or should be interpreted in specific fashions other than indicated by the auditory aspect. The
foreign student should be made to realize that this is the case and
that he should look for those visible aspects which inject meaningful nuances into the conversation. "Drop dead!" said with a
friendly grin is not to be interpreted in this society as an impreca-
tion of a curse upon the recipient.

Some sounds may appear acoustically correct but look incorrect. Relatively similar f's may be made by modifying the outgoing breath stream in either of two major ways: by gently approximating the upper front teeth and lower lip in such a manner
that a frictional noise is produced, or by approximating the lower
front teeth and the upper lip. The former technique is preferred
in English, and is readily noted by most foreign students. Sur-

prisingly enough, however, many foreign students and American stutterers ignore the *gentle* component of the teeth-lip contact and pull the lower lip up under the superior teeth for a prolonged, hard contact. This distorts both the quality and duration of the sound, and indirectly, the rhythm of the phrase. Here, the use of a mirror is quite beneficial. Both teacher and student should be visible in the mirror at the same time so that the student may alternately observe his instructor's and his own articulatory movements. While still using the mirror, the student should make the sound in isolation and then in several sound combinations. As a supplementary assignment, he should observe and tabulate *f* productions of individuals not in the class.

V, which, with the exception of vocal cord vibration, is produced much like *f*, is commonly mispronounced by foreign students. Some Spanish speakers approximate both upper and lower lips while producing a sound similar to *v*, and are unaware that they are producing a non-English sound. Partial unvoicing and shortening of the *v* by speakers of germanic and slavic languages is frequently encountered. The acoustic end-products are so subtly different from their equivalent sounds in the speaker's native languages that the instructor needs to combine auditory and visual training techniques to make the student aware of the differences. In general, it takes longer for the student to master English sounds which are subtly dissimilar from those of his native language than it does to master grossly different phonemes.

In addition to the confusion of *f* with *v*, many of the same students substitute *v* for *w*, and occasionally, *w* for *r*. English *w* and *r* at the beginning of words cannot be taught in isolation because they cannot be made alone. One may define the *w* as a transition from purse-string puckered lips into a vowel or vowel-like sound. It is the tensing lip projection before the vowel that gives the characteristic *w* impression. In the *r*, there is also lip projection prior to the vowel, but there is noticeably less tense, purse-string movement than in *w*. Again, the differences are subtle, but significant. It is especially important that the tip and blade of the tongue not touch the upper teeth, gum ridge, or roof of the mouth in *r* production.

Confusions between *m* and *n* are occasionally encountered and may be solved by demonstrating that one closes the lips for *m* and opens them for *n*. Slight mouth opening combined with medial tongue placement are primary cues for the two *th* sounds as in *thin* and *the*. *Th's* are so frequently mispronounced by foreign students (and many native Americans) that the neophyte teacher nearly always starts with them because even the student is usually aware that he makes the *th*'s improperly. Yet, in terms of meaning, there is rarely any semantic confusion caused by imperfect *th* production. Where the student has difficulty in speech communication, it is perhaps more valuable to begin with vowel and diphthong production, for much more learning of vocabulary and pronunciation is liable to ensue from emphasis on vowels and diphthongs than from concentration of *th*. There is also the strange embarrassment of many foreign students when requested to protrude their tongues. While studying in Europe I first observed that many Europeans and Asians whom I encountered appeared ashamed of their teeth and barely opened their mouths. Several years later, one of my Filipino friends who had a Ph.D. in Linguistics from one of our better-known American universities admitted that she had never looked at a tongue, even in her graduate training, because in her country it was considered ill-bred to show the tongue.

Coupled with the cultural orientations referred to above, there is another form of embarrassment reflected in insufficient mouth opening. Some students are shy and hesitate to speak. They may often hold their jaws relatively rigid, which in turn muffles the speech. With this restricted jaw activity, the tongue does not have enough freedom to move efficiently through its articulatory duties. Mildly hard-of-hearing students who have sensorineural hearing problems may hold the teeth together so that they may feel the vibrations better. Those whose hearing losses are temporary or non-neurological in nature may hear themselves too loudly because outside sounds appear fainter; therefore they may speak softly and with overall reduced vigor of articulatory motion.

Whatever the cause, the student should become aware of the benefits of mouth opening. Here, again, the mirror is excellent for demonstrating the visual differences that accompany acoustic differences. The *aw* in *paw* is easily distinguished from the *o* in *no,* the *oo* in *too,* and the *ah* in *pa* by degrees of mouth opening and lip-rounding. *E* in *yes* and *ee* in *see* differ slightly in tongue height. The back of the tongue may come slightly farther forward in the mouth for the vowel in *cat* than it does for the *ah* which is its usual substitute.

Mirror practice by the student and teacher may be effectively supplemented by having students with similar problems work on each other before the mirror. The expedient of turning the student into a teacher often increases the rapidity of learning.

As soon as possible, the student should learn to perform while in a standing position. This is less inhibiting than always performing while seated, and contributes to more forceful, dynamic speech.

CHAPTER VI

KINESTHETIC–PROPRIOCEPTIVE TRAINING

Kinesthesia AND *proprioception* are terms which refer to sensations of tension, position and movement of various parts of the body as perceived through nerve endings in muscles, tendons and joints, in other words, feelings which accompany physical movements. These feelings are part of the sensory feedback system which helps the body to monitor and self-correct its actions, just as organs of hearing, sight and smell help the over-all body to reorient itself and act in response to new stimuli. Each time a baby learns new gross physical coordinations or a professional baseball pitcher refines the delivery of a curve ball, each time an aspiring ballerina masters a new posture or a trout fisherman increases the skill with which he flicks his hook at a spot in the water, kinesthesia and proprioception are at work. When the labored printing of the school child evolves into a flowing legible script the muscular feedback system is largely responsible for the change. As your eyes follow the line you are now reading, this same feedback system determines in part the number of fixations your eye muscles will make, and will have participated in your having learned to read English print from left to right rather than from right to left, top to bottom or bottom to top as in other languages. This same system is active in speech.

In discussing the speech mechanism, it is convenient to subdivide it into: 1) *cerebration;* 2) *respiration;* 3) *phonation;* 4) *resonance;* and 5) *articulation. Cerebration* refers to activity of the brain, whether conscious or unconscious, and includes messages going to and from the brain via nerves as well as associational messages going from one part of the brain to another. Thus it participates in the activities of the other subdivisions. *Respiration* deals with the muscular activity of getting air into the lungs and waste-laden air out of the lungs. It also has chemical and biological duties involving transmission of oxygen and other gasses through various body tissues. *Phonation* designates the role of the vocal folds and associated parts of the larynx in the production of voice by interrupting the outgoing breath stream. *Resonance* is the name given to the processes wherein the throat, mouth and nasal cavities interact to change the characteristics of the sounds generated at the vocal fold level so that various vocal qualities are produced. *Articulation* embraces the movements of teeth-bearing jaws, tongue, soft palate, and throat walls which result in the alteration of the outgoing air stream into different sounds. In my thinking, the actions of the vocal folds help us to discriminate one sound from another (*f* from *v*, *t* from *d*, *k* from *g*, *s* from *z*, etc.) and should lead us to classify the vocal folds among the articulators. Since the opening and closure of the vocal folds partially regulates inhalation and exhalation of air, they may also be considered part of the respiratory system. Similarly, movements of the articulators alter the resonance of sounds, which might permit us to say that articulators and resonators may each be classified under the other. The breakdown into the above five categories is thus obviously quite arbitrary since all interact in an amazingly complex fashion. Yet, for pedagogical purposes, the five categories simplify explanations.

In previous chapters which related to the use of auditory and visual feedback as part of the language training process, there was constant reference to positions of the articulators as related to auditory and visual cues. Such references to articulatory positions were usually in accord with standard views as presented in phonetics texts. Recent research by MacPherson (1968) has shown that many people who are considered normal speakers of CAE do not articulate according to text book descriptions, yet are perfectly comprehensible. A wide variety of tongue and jaw movements, for instance, result in acceptable *l*'s as in *la-la-la-la-la*. Jann, Ward and Jann (1964) report accoustically normal *l*'s produced with the tongue protruded.

Why is it that different people produce similar sounds with such different articulatory movements? We don't really know yet and can only guess that the cerebrative (hearing, associational and motor sub-divisions), articulatory and resonatory mechanisms interact to alter the physical structures so that equivalent sounds may result. One implication of the results of these studies may be that the teacher or therapist should try traditional techniques of tongue placement and other standard articulatory techniques, but that if these prove fruitless, and if the student should happen upon a correct sound production by chance or by auditory stimulation, the student should be encouraged to repeat the sound and to develop a physical feeling which he associates with that specific sound. His visible physical movements and those he reports may not remotely agree with textbook definitions and descriptions, and the teacher may not be able to produce the same sound employing the technique used by the student, but perhaps that technique may work with another student. Teachers often learn a great many useful pedagogical techniques from their students.

Some students are more aware than others of their articulatory movements and positions. Merely demonstrating or discussing appropriate movements may aid a few students to alter their coordinations so that correct sounds ensue. Others may need combined mirror work and/or auditory stimulation. Still others may need to sensitize their tongue tips by biting them, by sucking spicy candy, or by pricking the tongue with a tooth pick or other sharp object. One convenient technique is to place a minty or spicy life-saver type of candy between the teeth and then rub the tongue against it to irritate the tip.

Another technique developed by Young and Hawk (1955) is for the teacher or therapist to manipulate the student's articulators. They have successfully used this approach with students who had articulatory problems of a functional nature as well as with stutterers, aphasics, mentally retarded children, deaf and hard of hearing children and adults.

The Tadoma approach to teaching speech to deaf or blind children (K. Alcorn, 1938; S. Alcorn, 1941) may be adapted to the needs of the foreign student. In essence, in this approach the student closes his eyes and gently places his hand on the teacher's face in such a way that his three middle fingers may gently touch the cheek and nose, and the thumb the lips, and the small finger the neck in the area of the larynx. While the teacher speaks, vibrations may be felt by one or more of the fingers. The student then tries to duplicate the vibrations or sense of movement. A variant of this approach is for the teacher to place the back of the student's hand a few inches from the teacher's mouth so that the student may feel the force, direction and duration of the teacher's breath for a specific sound or syllable.

For obtaining better resonance, both direct and indirect techniques may be tried. A simple exercise previously discussed is to increase vertical mouth opening. This, coupled with gentle, prolonged inhalation, usually produces a cool feeling in the back of the throat while at the same time causing the back of the tongue to lower and the throat walls to expand, thus altering the shapes and sizes of those resonators. Various relaxation devices ranging from conscious muscular limpness through reassurance, humming, singing, semantic relaxation, Yogi methods and others may reduce inhibiting muscular tension so that better coordination of speech muscles may occur.

Nearly two hundred muscles—perhaps more—may go into action for the utterance of any one speech sound. Their coordinated interactions vary in some degree from one sound to another. The possible number of muscular patterns of interaction is so large that we may consider it a near miracle that anyone learns to speak in a consistently coordinated comprehensible manner at all. Therefore, one should be neither surprised nor disappointed if it takes a student more than just a few minutes to overcome years of practice in using speech muscular habit patterns which are inappropriate to the excellent pronunciation of a second language.

CHAPTER VII

USE OF CONTEXT

W ORDS BY THEMSELVES generally convey little meaning, with the exceptions of one-word commands, answers to questions, or perhaps conventional sociable short utterances. Examples of these would be the military maneuver commands of *halt!, attention!*; the versatile *stop!, wait!, listen!, yes, no, maybe, well, fine, hello, good-bye,* and similar one-word responses. Words grouped together into meaningful phrases are much more commonly utilized in CAE to achieve communication. The addition of feeling-tone via vocal quality, facial movements and gestures further enlivens phrases, and when these enlivened phrases are the natural products of a contextual situation the sense of communication is much nearer to completion.

Granted, there are some individuals who can imbue one word with a phenomenal amount of meaning, but such speakers are rare in this society. Jack Benny's consummate use of the word *well!* is a case in point, but Mr. Benny is known for evolving his humor from stereotyped behavior and *situation comedy* wherein one episode builds upon another to culminate into a series of laughable absurdities. If one were not to begin to pay attention to a Benny sketch until it had progressed for a few minutes it would take a short time to shake off a feeling of disorientation so that the humor would have meaning. The scene needs to be set so that the audience can follow the logical sequence of ideas and events and react as the writers and players had planned. Daily conversations are very much the same way.

It is the rare individual who can join a conversational group and immediately follow and enter into the discussion unless the group members pause and focus the attention upon the new arrival. Possibly, he may interrupt the discussion to express an urgently felt need. The foreign student seldom follows the latter approach. He is more likely to listen on the periphery of the conversation until a timely pause occurs or until he is recognized and invited to participate. The natural reticence of a stranger to obtrude upon a group or to phrase questions concerning what had been discussed prior to his arrival may lead to a lack of orientation similar to what a native American may feel when he only hears the last part of a joke and can't understand why everyone around him is laughing. If he has heard the joke before, the punchline alone may be sufficient to bring out of his memory those associations which provide immediate orientation. Sophisticated speakers of a language can often pick up the thread of a conversation rapidly because it follows a pattern familiar to them, just as the sophisticated joke-listener may rapidly recognize the pattern of a joke or story. The foreign student lacks such sophistication and awareness of the types of normal patterns of conversational presentation. Humor, which is customarily couched in colloquial or idiomatic terms and which frequently leans on puns, is even more difficult to follow.

It becomes important, then, to present new material to a foreign student contextually so that: 1) he becomes oriented to the new material as soon as possible; 2) he perceives patterns of speech behavior which eventually become predictable; 3) he becomes securer in his ability to learn and retain new language and speech concepts, and 4) he begins to feel "at home" with his new language.

A useful approach to the teaching of vocabulary and pronunciation is to work in categories. It is easiest to begin with a category which might be entitled *The Class Room*. Words and their appropriate phrases or sentences may be built around the persons and things in the room and actions concerning them. The teacher may say, pointing to a door, "That's a door." The student attempts "That iss a door." The teacher then corrects him, explaining that *that* and *is* are combined into one word—*that's*, and *a* is pronounced *uh* in informal speech. This is drilled on to the teacher's satisfaction, after which he may teach several other phrases based on *door*, such as "Where's the door?" "There's the door." "Where is it?" "There it is." "I'm going to open the door." "You open the door!" "Where does that door go to?" After this, other aspects of the immediate environment may be drilled upon, as much as possible using similar phrasal patterns to those just studied. Since many of the same phrasal patterns which apply to *door* also apply to *window, window* would be a legitimate next word to use as the base for phrasal practice. More advanced students may be ready for categories such as sports, politics, fashions, magazines, social activities, dating, the home, family members, jobs, window shopping, restaurants, crime, war, travel, art and as many other topics as may be mutually interesting. The students are often willing to suggest categories, indeed, eager to do so, for many of their questions concerning vocabulary and customs may be best answered via this form of exercise.

Reading aloud is a technique used by many teachers. A short reading which is complete in a very few lines is preferred to longer passages. The teacher should explain the difficult and unfamiliar words prior to having the student drill on the phrasal pronunciation. The student should learn which words change pronunciation when they move from isolated to contextual situations, and be able to produce them accordingly. Although it is customary to start with simple phrasal and sentence patterns, it is not mandatory. Some relatively bizarre sentence patterns occur fairly frequently in CAE, and due to their frequency, are of great value in catching and holding the student's interest.

Poetry should be minimized in the early stages of speech training, for it does not usually represent colloquial patterns. It is best used in a memorized fashion to illustrate concepts of linking, rhymed pronunciation, rhythm, and stress. Key words in poetry may be especially labored over as referents for specific difficult pronunciation concepts so that the student may have his own personal mnemonic aids. Thus in the line—*The kite is high in the sky today, and a cloudy sky, I'd say*—various pronunciations of *i* and *y* and *a* are presented in a manner which allows the student to learn the pronunciations of these spellings and then to generalize from their pronunciations to those of other words which follow the same oral rules. Some generalizations from this line might be: 1) *i* followed only by a consonant and *e* has one pronunciation, but *i* followed only by a consonant has another pronunciation; 2) final *y* in a one-syllable word may or may not rhyme with the *i* in *kite,* but it is more likely to do so if preceded by a consonant, for a preceding vowel may radically alter its pronunciation. These generalizations may not be completely true, but they serve their purpose for the time and may be supplanted by fuller, more accurate information when the student is ready for it.

Short humorous stories which contain plays on words serve a double purpose. In addition to building vocabulary and pronunciation, they give insights into the kinds of humor Americans are supposed to appreciate, and help the student to become oriented to the patterns into which he may translate humorous stories of his own country. This may result in an exercise which requires the student to do just this—translate one of his favorite stories into CAE with the teacher's help, and carefully polish it so that he may present it either before the class or in a social situation.

Question and answer sessions based on daily activities, a category, or an immediate problem offer an opportunity to build conversational practice into a contextual exercise. At first, the student's participation may be somewhat stiff and stilted, but as his self-confidence grows he should become more and more daring. When the student attempts to tease the teacher during one of these give-and-take sessions, this should be taken as a sign that the student has progressed to the point where he no longer worries about the bare necessities of daily existence; now he is ready to socialize.

CHAPTER VIII

PERSONALIZING THE SUBJECT MATTER

STUDENTS ARE INDIVIDUALS with personal needs and interests. A good teacher will discover the needs and interests of his students and build them into lessons. Needs turn into interests because of the accompanying sense of immediacy, and working on the vocabulary and pronunciation aspects of these needs vitalizes the lesson. What may not ordinarily be taken into consideration by the teacher or the therapist might be of extreme immediate importance to the student. Such problems may include getting along with a roommate; ordering food in a restaurant; where to shop on a limited budget; how to meet Americans socially; what to do with a spouse who refuses to speak English.

The roommate situation may be turned into a lesson by covering dormitory regulations, terminology common to student dormitory life, suggestions on how to talk to counsellors and roommates. For ordering food in a restaurant, menus and introductory phrases such as "May I have an order of . . ." or cautionary remarks like "I'd like the steak very rare, please" prove quite helpful. If the class is small enough, a session or two may be spent in a restaurant with the teacher ordering first, and helping the student with the terminological phrasing.

Advice may be given on where to shop for specific items. This nearly always evokes a need for a certain vocabulary, which in turn requires pronunciation practice. If possible, field trips to stores should be taken, for the contents of stores are excellent visual aids which require less explanation than merely the names of the items without the visual referents.

Many foreign students tend to cling together for moral support and for social life, especially when several come from the same country as a group. This leads to a general retardation of their acquisition of English language and customs. Some colleges and universities unwittingly foster this situation by setting aside housing space exclusively for foreign student habitation. This is occasionally misconstrued as a manifestation of prejudice against foreign students and they respond accordingly. Where dormitory space is unavailable, they may group together and procure private housing. An unfeeling landlord may charge extravagant prices when aware of the students' relative ignorance of prevailing rental prices. In situations such as this, the student should be counselled to discuss the situation with the university offices whose responsibility it is to deal with foreign student affairs. If there is no such office, either supportive advice may be given or the teacher may decide to intervene.

Many foreign students are wives of former American servicemen or of Americans who have worked or studied overseas. When their family and social situations are acceptable to them, they have fewer problems than do other foreign students on the whole. But the newly-arrived bride whose husband is also new to this city may have even more difficulty in adjusting. For her, the class is liable to be one of her primary social activities, and could be a springboard into a happier home life. One of our students was a hard-of-hearing Italian woman married to a bi-lingual American of Italian parentage. The husband wanted their pre-school daughter to learn Italian first despite their intention to remain in this country. Therefore he suggested that only Italian be spoken in the home. The wife urgently desired to become Americanized, and since a hearing aid gave her sufficient hearing to pick up CAE pronunciation patterns, she was upset at not being able to practice speaking English at home. In this instance, it was decided that a family conference was necessary. When the husband was informed of his wife's feelings and of the difficulties which the child would face, it recalled to him similar difficulties he had encountered as a child whose immigrant parents spoke only Italian. He promptly did an about face and even arranged for his child to enroll in a speech clinic for English language training in a play therapy environment. It was suggested that the wife accompany the child to the therapy lessons and sit in on them in order to learn along with her daughter so that they might discuss their new common experiences in the new common language.

An Hungarian-born American citizen was ashamed that he could not read children's stories to his young daughter. The lessons in this case were slanted to the selection of good literature for children and to the reading aloud from his daughter's favorite books. Her school books were also used to provide discussion topics.

Students will often suggest lesson material if encouraged to do so. The day a controversial political figure was due to arrive on campus two students asked for information concerning him since they had been assigned to attend his speech in order to report upon it in another course. This led to a lively set of questions and answers resulting in nearly the entire class going to hear the speech and participate in the accompanying shenanigans. The speaker was a quite colorful, reactionary southern politician, so we drilled on words he was known to have used in his previous speeches and publicity releases. Therefore, when the topic of civil rights came up, the students had learned enough vocabulary to follow the speaker's train of thought. When they returned to class for the next lesson, they requested that they be allowed to discuss the speech, the over-all audience reaction, their individual reactions and similar situations in their own countries.

It is normal for the foreign student to be homesick when away from home in a land where he may feel isolated or neglected. Just talking about home may alleviate the nostalgia. For this reason, it is recommended that each student prepare a speech about some facet of life in his own country, such as his family, his home, his previous job, what he intends to do when he returns home, social customs and the like. This speech may be prepared at home or in class, but it is preferable to prepare it in class so that the other students may learn similar common phrases and pronunciations while watching and listening.

In my experience, the majority of foreign students are male, and many of these are bachelors. Depending upon their native countries, dating and moralistic standards may be quite different from those of the American community in which they are temporary residents. Unknowingly, at first, they encounter unfamiliar types of responses when they attempt to date an American girl.

Some unfortunate choices of terminology are in part responsible for this. Their own interpretation of the girls' frankness may be responsible for most of the other problems. South Americans, especially, are unaccustomed to the relative freedom which American girls enjoy, being more familiar with the *duenna* system which still exists in many parts of South America. They have been known to misconstrue this relative freedom to the point of getting their faces slapped. In class, this kind of problem may be discussed quite satisfactorily—even in a class where both sexes are present—for the female foreign student may also learn what is considered acceptable behavior for women in this country.

All of these topics—and many others—have vocabulary and pronunciation exercises which evolve from the subject matter. A lesson hastily contrived from felt needs such as those discussed above may be of infinitely more practical worth than one which has been laboriously prepared over a fairly long time period. However, it must be kept in mind that a degree of pre-planning and structure should be present so that the teacher's objectives, as well as the students' may be met.

CHAPTER IX

SUPPLEMENTARY SOURCES OF IDEAS
AND DRILL MATERIAL

By now, it should have become apparent that the previous chapters of this book did not completely discuss any of the main ideas in them. Rather, they were intended to orient the reader to the existence of general points of view which he might pursue as he desires. For some people a step-by-step, logical explanation is needed for the comprehension of a new concept. For others, merely a hint sets their minds actively racing on the intended track. For the former, these chapters may have been too skimpy, for the latter they may have been too verbose. In the present chapter, several general and specific supplementary sources will be indicated.

TYPES OF SOURCES

Obvious references would be those whose titles indicate that they are intended for teachers of English to the foreign-born. The national professional association primarily interested in this area is TESOL. This acronym stands for Teachers of English to Speakers of Other Languages. TESOL publishes a journal entitled *Tesol Quarterly,* which includes both philosophical articles and pedagogical techniques which have been tested by experienced teachers. The first issue (Volume 1, Number 1) was published in March, 1967.

TESOL is an outgrowth of a need for an organization dedicated especially to the teacher of English to speakers of other languages. Members of various organizations whose interests were in this area obtained the sponsorship of their organizations so that TESOL might come into being. These sponsoring organizations were the National Council of Teachers of English, the National Association for Foreign Student Affairs, the Speech Association of America, the Modern Language Association of America and the Center for Applied Linguistics. Some publications of these associations, therefore, contain useful information for teachers of foreign students.

TESOL also publishes a newsletter. The first issue (Volume 1, Number 1) is dated April, 1967. In this issue are advertisements by several publishing companies. Thomas Y. Crowell Company of 201 Park Avenue South, New York, New York 10003, offers the following:

> *English Sounds and Their Spellings.* by Allen, Allen and Shute
> *Contemporary Spoken English I* and *Contemporary Spoken English II,* by Institute of Modern Languages, Inc.
> *American Folktales I: A Structured Reader* and *American Folktales II: A Structured Reader,* by Binner.

Collier-MacMillan International, 866 Third Avenue, New York, New York 10022, recommends:

> *Audio-Lingual English: A Semi Self-Instructional Language Laboratory Program*
> *Drills and Exercises in English Pronunciation:* (Three books accompanied by 54 prerecorded tapes)
> *Special English* (A series of fifteen books and tapes providing vocabulary development in the English employed in a specific profession or business)

The American Book Company, 55 Fifth Avenue, New York, York, advertises complete programs for elementary school, high school and adults via four series of books, including:

> *We Learn English Series,* by Bumpass
> *We Speak English Series,* by Bumpass
> *Let's Learn English Series,* by Wright, McGillivray, Barrett and Van Syoc
> *Let's Write English,* by Wishon and Burks

The Regents Publishing Company, a division of Simon and Schuster, Inc., 200 Park Avenue South, New York, New York 10003, lists over fifty items under the heading of: Basic Courses, Grammar and Structure, Conversation, Comprehension, Readers,

Idioms, Pronunciation Workbooks, Pre-Recorded Tapes and Records, Teachers' Reference Books Materials for Spanish-Speaking Students, and other Titles. This company has been interested in texts for foreign students for many years. In 1947, Regents brought out Clarey and Dixson's *Pronunciation Exercises in English,* which has since been revised (1963). They will provide a complete catalog of their TESOL-oriented materials upon request.

Harper and Row, Publishers, 49 East 33rd Street, New York, New York, offer:

Guided Writing and Free Writing, by Robinson
Writing English: A Composition Text in English as a Foreign Language, by Ross and Doty
Language and Life in the U.S.A.: American English for Foreign Students, by Doty and Ross
Using American English, by Newmark, Mintz, and Hinely

The McGraw-Hill Book Company of New York City lists over twenty-five titles under the categories: Primary Level, Secondary Level, University and Adult Level, and Professional Books.

The University of Michigan Press, 615 East University, Ann Arbor, Michigan 48106, offers under the series title of English Language Institute Publications:

Linguistics Across Cultures, by Lado
Teaching and Learning English as a Foreign Language, by Fries

A sub-series entitled Intensive Course in English contains:

English Pronunciation
English Pattern Practices
English Sentence Patterns
Vocabulary in Context

Two books not advertised in the *TESOL Newsletter* but which have been helpful to speech therapists are Black's *American Speech for Foreign Students,* published by Charles C Thomas, Springfield, Illinois, 1963, and Prator's *Manual of American English Pronunciation,* published by Rinehart and Company, 232 Madison Avenue, New York, New York, 1957. Another text which is more philosophical than of an immediate-use nature is Chreist's *Foreign Accent,* 1964, one of the Prentice-Hall Foundations of Speech Pathology Series. The publisher's address is Englewood Cliffs, New Jersey.

A book which influenced me a great deal in my early days of working with foreign students and from whose author I personally absorbed many philosophies and techniques is Mayer's *Guide to Pronunciation,* Wayne State University Bookstore, Detroit, Michigan 1958. Much of this present book is due to Dr. Mayer's influence.

There are undoubtedly several other texts written for specialists in this field which have been omitted in these few pages, and scores of journal articles which are worthy of mention. However, the above-listed items should serve as an orientation.

Other types of books that might be of service are often ignored by formally trained linguists. Yet, many of the old elocutionary texts contain fascinating techniques and drill material that might easily be adapted to the modern teacher's needs. While perusing several nineteenth century and early twentieth century elocution and rhetoric books, I was impressed by the up-to-dateness of some of the recommended techniques and practice material.

The legitimate successors of the elocutionists were the specialists in oral interpretation, public address, voice and diction, theatre and speech pathology. Occasionally, in public address and theatre texts, one may find useful material for foreign students, but not as often as in books on oral interpretation and voice and diction. The discipline imposed during a course of oral interpretation is excellent for the teacher of foreign students, for through an emphasis on nuances of meaning the student of oral interpretation develops a heightened awareness of the multiple components of language.

Drill books of voice and diction or of voice and articulation seem to be produced by individuals who have been trained in the combined areas of general speech and drama, speech pathology and speech science. Their emphases vary with the vintage and training of the author and greatly resemble some of the nineteenth-century elocution and rhetoric texts in modern form. They often include forms for analyzing speech for deviant patterns; introductions to phonetics; superficial discussion of the anatomy and physiology of speech; lists of words, phrases and sentences for patterned drill; short readings of well-known passages chosen from those in the public domain; and exercises for improving the efficiency of the speech mechanism. The better ones include normal CAE pattern practice of phrases and sentences, and often present minimal word pairs for auditory training practice. For the naive teacher of foreign students, voice and diction texts might be an excellent starting point since they are usually written quite simply and clearly, and give many hints on how to work with people who have poor articulation, voice, rhythm, rate, pitch and intensity. Unfortunately, they rarely cover basic concepts of English language structure.

Fairbanks' *Voice and Articulation Drillbook* (Harper, 1960) is widely used throughout the United States. Other representative authors in this area are Akin, Anderson, Brigance and Henderson, Bronstein and Jacoby, Eisenson, Fisher, Hahn, Hargis, Lomas and Van Draegen, Karr and Van Dusen. Many authors of oral interpretation and speech pathology texts have published articles in journals of the Speech Association of America *(Quarterly Journal of Speech, Speech Monographs, The Speech Teacher)* and of the American Speech and Hearing Association *(The Journal of Speech and Hearing Disorders, The Journal of Speech and Hearing Research)* as well as in psychological, linguistic, and acoustical journals.

Speech pathology, as a relatively new field, has been borrowing and adapting ideas from a number of other professional disciplines such as speech and drama, clinical and experimental psychology, linguistics, anatomy, physics, education, education of the deaf, clinical medicine, anthropology, physical and vocational rehabilitation. Basic surveys of speech pathology as presented by Van Riper or by Johnson *et al.* are of some—although little—aid to the naive teacher of foreign students. Nemoy and Davis in *The Correction of Defective Consonant Sounds* (Expression Company, Magnolia, Massachusetts, 1948), present excellent moral support for the neophyte teacher or therapist via a detailed analysis of correct and incorrect consonant production, supplemented by copious drill material. Although slanted toward children, many of the Nemoy and Davis exercises may be employed effectively with foreign students. This book has gained a reputation for getting insecure new speech therapists through their first therapy sessions. Its relative weakness lies in the area of pattern practice on an adult level; its major strengths include auditory training practice and placement of the articulators.

Teachers of foreign languages to Americans face problems similar to those of the teacher who tries to teach CAE to a foreign student. Conversations with language teachers are recommended as a means of discovering ways of dealing with typical situations that arise in second language teaching. By working backward from the difficulties that an American student would have in learning a foreign language, many insights may be gained.

Vocal and instrumental music teachers may be of service, especially in the training of rhythm, pitch, rate and stress. Music teachers are often quite helpful both in musical techniques and in second language learning techniques since many serious students of music learn to sing in other languages.

Ideas and suggestions may come from a variety of sources. However, once you achieve a modicum of self-confidence, you should develop a tenable rationale for the teaching of CAE pronunciation in the framework of linguistic communication and cultural integration.

CHAPTER X

SAMPLE PROCEDURES

The Preliminaries

W HETHER WORKING with individual students or with a group, there are certain recommended preliminary steps. The first of these would be to set up a data or information file on each student. This need not be elaborate, but it should contain at least the following minimal information:

Name
Date of birth
Place of birth
Permanent address
Temporary address
Telephone number
Native language (s)
Years of training in the native language
Years of training in English
Years or months he has spoken English
Educational level in his native country
Previous profession
Present profession or major course of study
Intended profession after completion of training
Information on his family
Specific problems he complains of concerning his English
Your estimate of his English language difficulties
An indication of what training should be undertaken first

Other questions which would be important enough to note would include such points as:

Does he presently reside in an English-speaking domicile?
Does he have roommates who speak English?
Are radios or television sets easily accessible to him?

44

Does he have a tape recorder?
Does he have American friends, relatives or associates with whom he spends portions of each day?
If married, has he brought his spouse and/or children with him?
If he has a job, of what kinds of duties does it consist?
Does he have visual, auditory, mental or emotional problems?

If possible, a tape recording should be made of his speech at the first reading. The recording should contain samples both of reading and of conversational speech. These may be analyzed to provide a partial basis for future lessons and should be kept as a measuring stick with which the student may compare his progress. Such recordings usually show the student at his worst, so they help his morale later, for after he has had a few lessons and developed some confidence the "before" and "after" recording may be compared, revealing deceptively vast improvement.

In evaluating the speech and language of the student, two major sub-divisions should be considered: *communication* and *style*. Under communication, the following might be indicated:

Does he have trouble communicating his ideas to me? If so, how much trouble?

Do other people complain that he has difficulty communicating his ideas to them?

Has his poor English communication affected him adversely? How?

Does he understand what I say to him or does it appear that he merely tries to give the impression that he understands?

Does he understand formal English better than colloquial American English, *vice versa,* or equally?

Is his ability to comprehend written English good enough so that it may be used as a starting point or an aid to the speech training?

Does he demonstrate specific personality characteristics that might hinder or facilitate the learning processes?

Does he seem motivated to communicate and try to let others communicate with him?

To Prator (1957), communication is of paramount importance. Unfortunately, however, to many teachers style is of primary consideration. A good training program should stress both. Of what does *style* consist? It may include grammatical and syntactical structures, specific pronunciations, word choice, rhythm, rate, timing, stress and intonation. Therefore, under style, one may ask:

Is he consistent in his misuse of grammar and syntax?

Is he aware of the kinds of grammatical and syntactical errors he makes?

Can he be easily stimulated to correct such grammatical and syntactical errors, or are they so ingrained as habits that they will be more difficult to alter?

Does he appear to have an almost innate feeling for the correct choice of words, or does he merely grope for any vaguely applicable words?

Does he grasp or even care for the melody of American English, or is he at the stage where he is happy if he can utter a few disjointed words?

As an alternative, does he desire "stage" or Southern British pronunciation as a result of the training?

Does he have a "good ear," that is, can he differentiate one pattern or sound from similar ones?

In order of severity, what are his types of stylistic error?

The answers to the above and other questions on *communication* and *style* should be analyzed and weighed in some manner that the relative emphasis for a specific student's training may be slanted toward his most obvious needs. Once such questions are asked the program may be tailored for the individual student, and in the situation where there are several students, grouping may become easier on the basis of similarity of needs or levels of sophistication.

The logical, analytically-oriented teacher or therapist may wish to test any or all of the stylistic components in depth. If so desired, written passages containing all the sounds of English may be read aloud by the student while the teacher marks errors on a separate copy. So-called articulation tests are commonly used by speech therapists to identify the specific phoneme errors. Articulation tests are intended to give the student an opportunity to speak each sound in initial, medial and final phonemic context, e.g., *boy*, *football*, *cab*. There are several standard articulation tests on the market, but with very little sophistication the beginning teacher or therapist may construct his own. Prior to constructing the test, any modern textbook on phonetics may be consulted for sufficient background in phonetic terminology and concepts. Modern dictionaries and Kenyon and Knott's *Pronouncing Dictionary of American English* may be consulted for information concerning the International Phonetic Alphabet (IPA). The specific phonetic symbols employed are not important. Any phonetic or diacritical system will suffice as a framework provided that it be employed consistently. One major problem occasionally encountered when working with articulation tests is that correct and incorrect consonants are easier to identify than are vowels and diphthongs. Yet, the foreign student will tend to have more vowel and diphthong than consonant errors, so it becomes especially important to learn to listen for vowel and diphthong distortions, substitutions, omissions and insertions.

Poor word choice needs no specific test. It soon manifests itself in conversation. Rhythm, rate, timing, stress and intonation irregularities are easily noted by the semitrained listener, but may be analyzed more carefully by having the student and a good speaker-reader of American English both record the same passage. These recordings may then be compared for each of the subcategories by replaying them as many times as necessary. This is an excellent learning experience for the teacher and may also be used as a lesson structure for the student.

Auditory discrimination (see Chapter IV) should also be investigated. It may well be a predictor of success in learning stylistic characteristics of speech. Students with poor auditory discrimination may need extra intensive training in that area in order to ensure maximal progress.

SCHEDULING

All too often, scheduling has to be on a "catch as catch can" basis. This is not especially desirable but is often better than nothing. Optimally, there should be two or more short sessions daily to provide a relatively constant reminder to the student that he must concentrate on techniques of both communication and style. Even more often than twice a day would be desirable, but almost impossible for most students and teachers in the face of conflicting schedules. One effective compromise is to meet for fifteen minutes daily during the noon hour in addition to regularly-scheduled thirty-minute or hourly sessions. If the student is enrolled in an organized English or Foreign Students program in addition to the program of speech training, the speech lessons may be arranged to fall on days not devoted to English, again to keep the learning concepts before the student's attention. Another approach might be to schedule the speech lessons either directly before or directly after the English class so that the two would reinforce one another. One thing is certain: both the student and teacher will feel that insufficient time is scheduled for speech training, no matter how much it is.

CHAPTER XI

PHONETICS AS A TOOL

A KNOWLEDGE OF PHONETICS is useful to both the teacher and the student in the identification and correction of improperly produced sounds of colloquial American English. It is a means of focusing upon specific sounds and sound families (phonemes) whose erroneous pronunciations not only *sound* incorrect, but also alter the rhythmic pattern of speech. Extra energy applied to one sound consistently may establish a non-American pronunciation pattern.

There have been literally hundreds of books and articles written on arbitrary phonetic or phonemic systems. Speech sounds have been classified and sub-classified, explained and argued over. Many elaborate categories invented to serve specific purposes often take longer to learn than may be worthwhile for the individual who desires to make immediate practical application of the system. For our purposes it may be easier to think in terms of two gross, partially overlapping categories: 1) vowels and vowel-like sounds, and 2) consonants and consonant-like sounds.

VOWELS AND VOWEL-LIKE SOUNDS

Vowels and vowel-like sounds may be thought of as those which have in common two characteristics: 1) the vocal folds come together and are vibrated (*voiced*), and 2) there is minimal interference with the outgoing flow of air after vibration at the vocal fold level. Some of their more commonly used symbols and key words for their pronunciations are listed below:

SYMBOL	KEY WORD
*/i/	s*ea*t, m*e*, s*ee,* p*eo*ple
**/I/	s*i*t, h*i*m, rh*y*thm
*/e/ or /eI/	s*ai*l, s*a*me, gr*ea*t, ch*ao*s
/ɛ/	s*e*t, *e*leven, br*ea*d

49

**/æ/	sat, cap, sad, angry
/a/	sod, father, honest
*/ɔ/	saw, taught, thought, broad
/o/ or /oU/	soap, snow, bone
**/U/	stood, pull, would, wolf
/u/	suit, Susan, grew, blue, shoot, duel, do
**/uh (stressed) /	supper, blood, other, young
**/ə (unstressed) /	above, cushion, necessary, commence
**/ɝ (stressed) /	bird, further, learn, word, jerk, purr, err
**/er (unstressed) /	father, pursue, lizard, preference
/aI/	I, aisle, high, scythe, eye, my, buy, guide, lie
*/Iu/ or /ju/	fuel, beauty, chew, you, music, view, yew
/aU/	now, shout, hour
*/ɔI/ or /oY/	boy, royal, toil, Detroit

* Difficult for most foreign students
** Especially difficult for most foreign students

In various dialectical pronunciations may be found some less commonly-used but often-encountered American and British vowels and vowel-like sounds:

/a/ is perceived as being almost like /a/ and almost like /æ/. It may occur in such words as ask, orange and Boston in Eastern or Southern Speech.

/D/ is a Mid-Western and British variant of /ɔ/, and may be noted occasionally in wash, sought, and water.

/ɜ/ may be detected in British and Southern speech as a replacement for /ɝ/ in bird, further, etc. It is made with less tongue movement than /ɝ/.

CONSONANTS AND CONSONANT-LIKE SOUNDS

Compared with the vowels and vowel-like sounds the consonants and consonant-like sounds are more easily written in alphabetical symbols.

SYMBOL	KEY WORDS
/p/—voiceless (unvoiced)	pig, open, up
/b/—voiced	boy, table, cab
/m/—voiced	man, command, come

**/θ/—voiceless	*th*in, ari*th*metic, pa*th*
**/ð/—voiced	*th*e, fa*th*er, smoo*th*
/t/—voiceless	*t*oy, phone*t*ics, ba*t*
/d/—voiced	*d*og, *d*oo*dl*e, be*d*
/n/—voiced	*n*o, fu*nn*y, do*ne*
*/l/—voiced	*l*ove, fe*l*t, fa*ll*
/k/—voiceless	*c*an, pa*ck*et, la*ck*
*/g/—voiced	*g*o, ba*gg*y, dra*g*
*/f/—voiceless	*f*un, lau*gh*ing, wi*f*e
*/v/—voiced	*v*ery, pa*v*ement, sha*v*e
**/ng/—voiced	si*ng*s, shini*ng*
/s/—voiceless	*s*ee, fir*s*t, pa*ss*
*/z/—voiced	*z*oo, buzzing, shoe*s*
*/sh/—voiceless	*sh*oe, na*ti*on, slu*sh*
*/zh/—voiced	mea*s*ure, bei*g*e
**/tsh/—voiceless	*ch*urch, wat*ch*ing
**/dzh/—voiced	*j*u*dg*e, ba*dg*er, wa*g*er
**/r/—voiced	*r*un, ma*rr*y, ca*r*
*/w/—voiced	*w*e, some*w*one
*/j/—voiced	*y*es, milli*o*n
*/h₁/—voiceless	*h*orse, top*h*at
*/h₂/—voiced	a*h*ead

---

* Difficult for most foreign students
** Especially difficult for most foreign students

/p/ as in *p*ig, o*p*en and u*p* is not voiced. At the beginning of a word or phrase it, as well as /t/ and /k/, tends to explode more than in medial or final positions. Foreign students seldom realize these positional explosion differences, which, in effect, alter the stress pattern of the language.

/b/ as in *b*oy, ta*b*le and ca*b* is similar to /p/, but is voiced and is sometimes longer in duration by a fraction of a second. Both /p/ and /b/ are exploded through the lips.

/m/ as in *m*an, com*m*and and co*m*e also utilizes the lips, but instead of the air being exploded through them as in /p/ and /b/, they remain closed while the air goes through the nose.

/θ/ as in *th*in, ari*th*metic, and pa*th* is unvoiced. The tongue approaches the front teeth gently while the lips and teeth are open. The tip is flattened so that a broad, flat, stream of air is squeezed between the tongue and the upper front teeth. There are many acceptable tongue positions for this sound.

/ð/ is the voiced cognate of /θ/. It is found in some of the most widely-used words in CAE: the, there, father, mother, other. As mentioned earlier, /θ/ and /ð/ are among the most difficult English sounds for foreign students to produce.

/t/ as in toy, bat and phonetics is the unvoiced cognate of /d/ as in dog, doodle and bed. The tongue presses against the upper teeth or gum ridge while air pressure builds up in the mouth cavity until the tongue is exploded free of the teeth or gums. The voiced /d/ may be slightly longer that the /t/. Medial /t/ as in little and bottle should normally sound almost like /d/. Foreign students may over-articulate medial /t/.

/n/ as in no, funny and done is voiced and has tongue positions similar to /t/ and /d/, but is not exploded. Rather, the voiced air goes through the nose.

/l/ as in love, felt and fall is described in many texts as having similar tongue positions to those of /t/, /d/, and /n/, but the voiced sound is released both over the sides and/or tip of the tongue with little pressure of an explosive nature. There is some argument for /l/ to be considered vowel-like.

The unvoiced and voiced cognates /k/ and /g/ as in can, packet and lack, go, baggy and drag, are usually formed by explosive release of the back of the tongue from the soft palate and tonsillar area. The position of the tongue tip varies with the neighboring phoneme.

/f/ and its voiced cognate /v/ as in fun, laughing, and wife, very, pavement and shave, require that the lower lip and the upper teeth be gently approximated while the air stream is vibrated by their partial blockage effect.

/ng/ as in sings and shining is a mixture of the characteristics of /n/ and /g/, but more toward the /n/. Foreign students try to overpronounce the /g/ component by exploding the sound so that it resembles /k/. They should be trained to reduce the energy and prolong the /n/-like part.

/s/ and its voiced cognate /z/ as in see, first and pass, zoo, buzzing and shoes, are special problems for Scandinavians who may not recognize the existence of /z/ in medial or final positions. They may be taught to try for a buzzing in the throat (voicing) which occurs during /z/ but not for /s/. Tongue positions for /s/ and /z/ are quite variable, but two major positional orientations are explained below: 1) prepare to say /t/ with the tongue tip against the upper front teeth or gums, but let the air be squeezed gently over the tongue tip without explosion; 2) place the tongue tip against the bottom part of the lower front teeth while squeezing the air between the middle of the humped tongue and the roof of the mouth.

/sh/ as in *sh*oe, na*ti*on and slu*sh* presents occasional problems, as does its voiced cognate /zh/ as in mea*su*re and bei*g*e. An almost squared, slightly trumpet-like projection of the lips helps to lend recognition to these sounds. The direction of the frictional modulation of air passing over the tongue and between the teeth varies with the preceding and following sound positions.

/tsh/ as in *ch*ur*ch* and wa*tch*ing combines characteristics of /t/ and /sh/, with the lip position of /sh/ often accompanying or even preceding, in some instances, the tongue position for /t/. The voiced cognate /dzh/ as in ju*dge* and ba*dg*er is often perceived as being slightly longer than the unvoiced /tsh/. Many foreign students tend to unvoice /dzh/ and to omit the /t/ aspect of /tsh/.

As with /l/, there may be sufficient argument for the following sounds to be classified as either vowel-like or consonant-like: /r/ as in *r*un, ma*rr*y and ca*r*; /w/ as in *w*e and some*o*ne; /j/ as in *y*es and mill*i*on, and the slightly voiced /h₂/ in a*h*ead. Each of these sounds is voiced, but the tongue, teeth and lips provide minimal obstruction to the air stream. None of these sounds is customarily capable of being made in isolation; they seem to be products of transitions between articulatory target positions, the /r/ resulting when moving to or from a relaxed pucker, the /w/ from a tense pucker, and the /j/ from near the /i/ positions. The unvoiced /h/ as in *h*orse and top*h*at, however, by virtue of not being voiced is arbitrarily lumped among the consonants. Its almost cognate /h₂/, which apparently occurs primarily when located between voiced sounds, may not be significant enough to argue over, but has been brought up here for discussion because it is commonly unvoiced and over-breathed by so many foreign students. One of the greatest problems foreign students have in learning /r/ is in overcoming their feeling that /r/ is a consonant and should be pronounced with the articulators impeding the air stream—which should *not* be the case in CAE. There should be no stoppage of the air flow above the vocal fold level. Another of their difficulties in learning the /r/ consists of concentrating on relaxing the lips while at the same time altering the tongue activity. A Japanese student, for example, mastered appropriate tongue action but his lip quivered as he strove to break up lip tensional patterns of improper /r/ production.

Rarely do students have difficulty in producing an acceptable /w/. Their major problems appear to lie in the area of when to use it rather than /f/, /v/ or other phonemes.

This chapter is merely an introduction to one orientation toward phonetics. It is recommended that you study one or more modern phonetics texts for other points of view so that you may feel more competent and sure of your ability to work with foreign students.

It is important for the beginning students of phonetics to realize that no phonetic system is accurate, valid, or very reliable. Any phonetic system you may encounter or use should be considered only a tool—a pedagogical instrument—and should be employed in as practical a manner as possible.

CHAPTER XII

INDIVIDUAL THERAPY

T HE AVERAGE BEGINNING teacher or therapist will usually start with one foreign student at a time in order to slowly work his way into a new type of teaching situation. For many, this individual interaction is valuable in that: (1) it helps to develop one's own confidence in what he is doing; (2) it is a means of ascertaining the feasibility and utility of the techniques; (3) it affords an opportunity to become oriented to the problems faced by the student and the teacher in attempting to achieve communication, and (4) it forces the teacher to look at his own language with new eyes and to hear it with newly focused ears. Let us pursue this concept a bit further.

When a speaker of another language asks an average, well-educated American to explain rules for certain pronunciations or translations he expects the American to have answers. The typical American usually has not thought of these questions before, or has not been bothered by the concepts involved since he was in elementary school. He may be able to provide a satisfactory answer from his stockpile of information, but more probably will have to reason out an explanation that will be acceptable both to himself and to the student. What often occurs is a discovery or re-discovery of the challenge of understanding his own language. His attempts to find easily understood and satisfactory explanations of the vagaries of American English force him to analyze it meaningfully for perhaps the first time in his life. He is compelled to look at his own language from the outside, to familiarize himself with it well enough so that he may conduct a guided tour through it. The mental gyrations involved in relearning his language from a different point of view, and then of developing techniques for communicating his knowledge to a person who has difficulty understanding him, stimulate both logical and creative thinking. He suddenly becomes aware of linguistic relationships which had never been taught him. His trial and error attempts teach him his capabilities and inadequacies. He learns that sincere interest in communicating with the student is more important than any specific techniques, that if he provides encouragement and moral support the student may soon blossom just because someone cares. For these reasons I feel that a native speech therapist should be offered the opportunity to work with foreign students early in his career. One foreign student is equivalent in problems to a wide variety of speech-defective Americans. He has more different articulation problems than ten children with moderately defective articulation. He may have problems in rate, rhythm, intensity, quality and variety equal to more than a half-dozen stutterers or voice cases. His communication problems in many ways resemble those of some aphasic or hard-of-hearing children. Techniques useful for therapy of diverse types of speech defectives may be applied to the foreign student, and some approaches that the therapist may invent for the foreign student are generalizable to other individuals with speech defects.

Additionally, the therapist learns to modify his own expressive language so that confusion is diminished. He learns that the process of verbal communication has certain commonalities to be considered and mastered regardless of the intellectual level of the communication. This is good practice for working with children.

Therefore, this chapter is dedicated to activities to be employed with a single student. Some of these may be applied—at least in principle—to groups. These lessons are not intended to be adhered to in a slavish manner, but rather are advanced in order to give the teacher or therapist a lifesaver to clutch at while the panic subsides enough for him to learn how to swim by himself.

THE INITIAL INTERVIEW

"The first time is the hardest." Many of the old saws are not necessarily true, but this one is nearly always applicable to second language teaching. For the student as well as the teacher, the first interview is liable to be an emotional experience, tinged with anxiety and self-doubts. By virtue of his relative authority, it becomes the duty of the teacher to set the student at ease. Doing so is not difficult. A friendly smile and greeting, followed by a short statement of being happy to meet him will often do the trick. Informal conversation and questioning may be employed to elicit the information which was discussed in Chapter Ten. This is the time for the teacher to discover what the student would like to learn, for the student should already know the areas in which his major problems occur. His explanations may provide the basis for much of the work to be done, not only with him, but with other students.

Beginning teachers need some form of structured lesson or overall format. After the case history is taken, a screening or evaluative step may follow. This may be informal, formal, or both. An informal assessment may include conversation, having the student describe the present room or explaining his reason for being in the United States. A moderately formal test would be to have him read aloud a short prose passage from a popular magazine or similar source which he would then be expected to paraphrase. As an alternative, the teacher could read one or more passages aloud and then ask the student several questions based on the reading. Some examples follow:

> George was sitting comfortably in the armchair, watching television. He wasn't especially interested in the show, but he was bored and had nothing better to do. In the middle of a commercial the telephone rang. As he got up to answer it, he tripped over an electrical wire and knocked over a lamp. The bulb shattered, and pieces of broken glass bounced along the floor. When George picked up the receiver of the telephone and said "Hello!" no-one answered. He quickly hung up the receiver. Then he straightened up the lamp, and with an old broom, swept up the glass. When he had emptied the fragments of glass into a waste basket, he looked critically around the room and decided that it needed a thorough cleaning—tomorrow. He returned to the armchair and television.

Questions:
1. What was the man's name?
2. Where was he sitting?
3. Did he enjoy the television show he was watching?

4. When did the telephone ring?
5. What happened when George went to answer the telephone?
6. Who called George on the telephone?
7. What kind of broom did George use?
8. Where did George put the broken light bulb?
9. Did George clean the entire room?
10. How did the story end?

It was dinner time at the Johnson house. Good smells drifted from the kitchen throughout the house. Mrs. Johnson and her oldest daughter, Sylvia, had just finished setting the table. Seven large plates were on the table. Napkins and forks were at the left of each plate. Knives, teaspoons and tablespoons were at the right. Two pairs of salt and pepper shakers were in position. There were no rolls this evening, but both white and whole wheat bread were on the bread plate. Since there was company for dinner, the usual margarine was replaced by butter. After the chicken, potatoes, peas, beets and salad were set on the table Mrs. Johnson reminded Sylvia to bring out the glasses and water.

Questions:

1. Who set the table?
2. How many people were going to eat?
3. Where were napkins and the knives?
4. How many salt shakers were on the table?
5. What did the Johnsons usually put on their bread?
6. Name the foods that were on the table.
7. What were they going to drink?

The two examples just given are of moderate difficulty. It is advisable to have some easier passages for people who might be at a lower level of ability.

The boy's name is Jim. Jim is a small boy. He is seven years old. He lives with his mother and father in a small house in the village. Jim has a dog. The dog's name is Spot. Jim and Spot are good friends.

Questions:

1. What is the boy's name?
2. Is Jim a big boy?

3. How old is Jim?
4. Where does he live?
5. Who is Spot?

Jim and Spot walked down the main street of the village. It was noon. The summer sun was very hot. Jim stopped in front of a building where automobiles were for sale. Spot stopped, too. There were several cars and trucks in the building. Some were red, some were blue, some were black, and some were green. Jim liked a red convertible best. He wished that his father would trade their old black sedan for the red convertible.

Questions:
1. What time of day was it?
2. What season of the year was it?
3. Where did Jim and Spot stop?
4. What did Jim and Spot see in the building?
5. Which car did Jim like best?
6. What kind of car did Jim's father have?
7. What did Jim wish?

Written passages akin to the above may be found in many magazines and books. These may be copied on separate sheets for either the student or the teacher to read, or the passages may be marked in the magazine or books for informal use. It takes little practice to learn how to make up questions appropriate to the text and the student. Periodicals like *Reader's Digest* contain materials on several levels within each issue, and are excellent sources since they contain a wide variety of subject matter as well. *Reader's Digest* also publishes a graded series of *Skill Builders* specifically intended to develop reading comprehension and vocabulary skills in a progressive manner. These are useful for evaluation, teaching, and for providing numerous topics for conversation and drill.

For more formal evaluation there are several possible procedures. Some of these are:
1. Reading aloud a passage for phonetic evaluation;
2. Recording of spontaneous speech for phonetic and structural analysis;
3. Administration of an "Articulation Test";

4. Administration of an "Auditory Discrimination Test";
5. Assessing auditory memory.

1. Reading aloud a passage for phonetic evaluation

In this procedure, it is necessary to have several lines of reading material which contain all or the majority of the sounds of CAE in their usual contexts. This means that any one spoken sound should be found in several combinations rather than just once. For example, *s* should be found at the beginning of a word before a vowel, but also before a consonant, after a vowel and after a consonant, as well as between two other sounds. When such a passage is found or invented it should be typed and, if possible, several copies should be made of it. The copies to be used as evaluation sheets should be double- or triple-spaced so that the evaluator may write his comments directly on the sheet in whatever code he employs. For a partial example, see below:

/tsh//tsh//vas//i//i//k//a//-/   /i//d//am/   /v//i//k/
1) George *was* sitting comfortably in *the* armchair, *watching*
/e/ /efizion/
    television.   2) He wasn't especially interested in the
    show, but he was bored and had nothing better to do. 3) In
    the middle of a commercial the telephone rang. 4) As he got
    up to answer it, he tripped over an electrical wire and knocked
    over a lamp.

From the first line, it is possible to see a pattern emerge. The /dzh/ sounds at the beginning and end of *George* were unvoiced. /v/ was substituted for /w/ in *was* and *watching*, but /f/ was substituted for /v/ in *television*. /i/ was consistently substituted for /I/ in *sitting, in, watching,* and *television*. In words ending in *ing* which would normally be pronounced /ing/, /ink/ was substituted (*sitting, watching*). Further checking this first sentence reveals difficulty with several other sounds. After awhile it becomes relatively easy to predict the sounds on which a given speaker will have difficulty, for they fall into patterns. Right now, try to predict the errors the student would probably make in lines 2, 3, and 4.

The passage should be read aloud once more so that problems in intensity, stress and timing may be noted.

2. **Recording of spontaneous speech for phonetic and structural analysis**

The teacher should practice with the tape recorder before trying it with a student. The tape or other recorder is set to record at a comfortable loudness level, with the microphone unostentatiously placed near the student. If possible, the microphone and the tape recorder should not be on the same table or equipment stand, for the machine may cause the table to resonate in such a way that it vibrates and produces additional background noise. An absorbent pad or a few newspapers between the machine and the table may be quite helpful. If space arrangements are such that the microphone and recorder are on the same table, similar padding between the microphone and the table would be recommended. Since recorders and microphones tend to have their own peculiar problems, two recorders of the same brand may perform dissimilarly, necessitating different settings on the loudness control and distance from microphone to speaker.

In selecting conversation for analysis, it is usually best to choose the first few utterances recorded, since it is common for these to be hesitant and stilted if the student is unaccustomed to microphones and to being recorded. If the topic is somewhat contrived, the conversation is likely to appear artificial, so it might be best to analyze specimens of conversation which contain real attempts at meaningful communication. Such segments may be replayed several times while either the teacher alone or both teacher and student note typical errors and patterns. After several times through these segments, the teacher may desire to categorize the types of errors, classifying them under appropriate phonetic, grammatic, syntactic, and other sub-headings. Analyses of this nature serve to establish areas where remediation may be useful, and often flow almost spontaneously into practical exercises. At least, they permit the teacher to list some of the student's specific problems for him so that he may begin to work on definite difficulties during the first meeting.

3. Administration of an "articulation test"

Speech therapists tend to rely a great deal—perhaps too much—on their own or published tests of articulation. The typical articulation test used by therapists on American children consists of having the child give the name of a pictured object. In some tests, the child repeats words after the therapist. In practically all instances, the average beginning therapist focuses primarily upon consonant production and skimps in the area of vowels. With foreign students, however, vowels are extremely important and should be evaluated extensively. Some information may be derived from the tests in which the student gives a one-word response like *horse* to a picture of a horse, but more may be learned if a carrier phrase precedes the response. Since a word in isolation is always stressed, component sounds may be distorted in a one-word answer, but if the student says *That's a horse* or *This is a horse or I think its a horse,* the pronunciation should be more representative of how he would use the word conversationally. Some therapists who use pictures prefer to have the student tell a short story about what he sees in the picture, eliciting such statements as these:

"In my country there are many horse. When I boy I ride horse. My father got farm."

or

"I like horses. My friend and I, we go to races many times."

or

"One time a horse bite me."

These contextual statements require very little more time than do one-word responses, but add immeasurably to the flavor of the interview. They often provide much information about the student's interests, likes, dislikes, misconceptions and emotional states. Picture articulation tests may be manufactured quite easily. It is common procedure for beginning students of speech therapy to list the vowels and consonants they desire to test and then rummage through old magazines and catalogs for pictures which contain the sounds in various positions. The cut-out pictures are then pasted to uniformly-sized cards (usually no larger than 5" x 8") with no more than three or four pictures per card. These may be used as separate cards or they may be combined into a book by encasing them in plastic inserts in an album intended for photographs, or by punching holes in the cards and inserting them into a loose-leaf binder. Score sheets may be composed and cheaply duplicated. Some therapists prefer to have separate sheets for vowels and consonants while others make up sheets only for consonants and note defective vowels by underlining or encircling the letters of the words printed on the form. It is customary in speech therapy types of evaluations to use some kind of code to indicate that sounds may be omitted, distorted, substituted or inserted. A dash (−) or "om" may stand for an omission; "dis" or a wavy line or many other symbols may signify distortion. When a sound is substituted for the preferred sound, the incorrect phoneme (if representable by a symbol) may be written down. A slash sign (/) between the sound made and the correct sound is occasionally used, so that when, for example, /k/ is substituted for /g/, it might be written k/g. Unnecessary insertions may be indicated by writing them on the form in the position in which they occur. When working with foreign students, it is advisable to invent or adapt additional symbols to indicate that a sound was overly exploded, prolonged, shortened or only partially pronounced. It is challenging to determine shorthand techniques for indicating these nuances, while at the same time not duplicating either phonetic symbols or those signifying omissions, distortions, substitutions or insertions.

Another form of articulation test which is often administered to older children, adolescents and adults is in a sentence form, with each sentence heavily loaded with the sound being evaluated:

1. *A*lice h*a*d H*a*nk's b*a*nd*a*na wr*a*pped around the *a*ngry sl*a*sh on her *a*nkle (æ).
2. *R*ita and A*r*thur *r*aced a*r*ound their b*r*other's ca*r* (r).
3. K*i*ck *i*t qu*i*ckly w*i*th the t*i*p of your toe (I).

This is an easy type of test to construct, and even easier to borrow from a voice and diction, linguistics or speech pathology text.

4. Administration of an "auditory discrimination test"

After some form of articulatory test has been given, it becomes desirable to learn whether the student is aware of his errors. One means of doing so is to see if he can distinguish between similar, but not identical, sounds. For example, if he said /vɔrs/ for *worse* the first two sounds were incorrect. When the teacher pronounces merely the two vowels, can the student tell whether they are similar or different? If so, can he then concentrate his listening sufficiently so that he can hear the difference between *worse* and *verse?* In other words, how well can he discriminate auditorily? When told to listen for fine differences does he learn to focus his hearing abilities? How long does it take for him to become oriented to this attitudinal set?

Although some therapists routinely administer a standard auditory discrimination test, there are many others who narrow discrimination testing to only the erroneous sounds produced during the informal and/or formal articulation testing. Either approach is acceptable, for a complete battery provides information to the therapist and listening practice for the student, and the error-based discrimination testing is only part of the continual appraisal and re-appraisal of which good therapy and teaching should consist. To a great extent, the amount of time available in the session may determine how much to do.

Rarely will students need such gross auditory discrimination testing and training as to indicate the relative loudness of a shout and a whisper. It is more customary to start with differences and similarities in phonemes within a word pair or a sentence pair, i.e., "Tell me if these two words sound the same or different: bear —pear. Good! Now let's try these pairs of words:

    talk—taught
    thick—sick
    come—come
    time—Tim
    fine—vine
    call—caw
    wine—vine
    take—cake

yes—yet
dare—there
jet—net
dine—dime
all—owl."

Six examples of sentence pairs were given in Chapter Four.
Here are some additional ones:

1. A. She fried some eggs in a pan.
   B. She fried some eggs in a man.
2. A. I like rice.
   B. I like lice.
3. A. Your jokes are very funny.
   B. Your jokes are very punny.
4. A. Shall we eat some chicken?
   B. Shall we eat some chicken?
5. A. I don't like Hugh.
   B. I don't like you.
6. A. What a silly tune!
   B. What a silly tone!
7. A. Tell me a story.
   B. Tell me a story.
8. A. Jump in the lake!
   B. Jump in the cake!
9. A. Let's buy a new coat.
   B. Lets' buy a new goat.
10. A. We should listen when he speaks.
    B. We should listen when he sneaks.
11. A. Where's John?
    B. Where's Jan?
12. A. On her head she wore a hood.
    B. On her head she wore a hod.
13. A. That apple is his.
    B. That apple is he's.
14. A. The carpenter has a strong voice.
    B. The carpenter has a strong vice.
15. A. The color black is associated with *caw*.
    B. The color black is associated with *car*.
16. A. He dropped his book.
    B. He dropped his brook.

17. A. I'm going to buy some wool.
    B. I'm going to buy some wood.
18. A. Take me home!
    B. Take me hum!
19. A. Give him this!
    B. Give him these!

The above sentences are all rather short. In each instance, the variable word is the last word in the sentence so that it may be presented smoothly as merely a part of the sentence. The different sounds should not be stressed during the testing procedure for the teacher needs to ascertain the student's present abilities in minimal auditory discrimination. If the same sentences are to be used in auditory training at a later time or even as part of the same session, then it is permissible, even recommended, to stress the differences as an initial part of the auditory focussing.

Another method of assessing auditory discrimination involves the use of the tape recorder. The teacher records a sentence or word. The student then records the same sentence or word. It is replayed one or more times while the student decides whether the two recordings are similar or different. This may be used as both a testing and a teaching technique. If the emphasis is to be on teaching, the instructor might select some "demon" words often mispronounced by foreign students to be included in this exercise. "Demon" words include most words with /I/, such as *it, him, his, this* (a double-demon because of the *th*), *hit, sit, swim, ring* (a triple-demon). /æ/ words are particularly frustrating: *am, at, hat, fan, sand, cat, dad, angry, apple, Alice, alcohol, pal, matter, match.* Words which contain both a *th* sound and /s/ or /z/ reduce some foreign students to tears: *this, those, these, soothe, smooth, thistle, thesis, theses.* For further difficult sounds and words, consult the two tables of vowels and consonants in Chapter Eleven.

5. Assessing auditory memory

In order for a person to be able to discriminate between two sounds, he must be able to remember the first sound long enough to compare it with the second. A nine-year-old child should be able to remember a string of as many as six or seven numbers or letters when he has heard them once: 3-7-2-8-1-4 or m-k-z-v-b-d. This is especially true when he knows the language well. He will not do so well when he has to perform the same type of task in another language because at least two more mental steps are demanded. Instead of: 1) listening; 2) remembering, and 3) repeating, he now must: 1) listen; 2) figure out what he has to remember; 3) remember; 4) figure out how he is to pronounce what he remembers, and then 5) repeat. Thus, if a foreign student performs well in this simple auditory memory test, it may predict that he will do relatively well in learning CAE with good pronunciation. To build up confidence, it is perhaps better to begin with short, easy sequences and build up to more difficult ones. Numbers alone, words representing the pronunciations of letters alone, nonsense words alone, short phrases, sentences, or diverse combinations thereof may comprise the test. As with all tests in this chapter, this test may be used as the basis for a lesson or series of lessons. Some sample series are:

one-two
three-four-eight
ten-five-nine
six-four-nine-two
seven-nine-six-one
twelve-nine-fourteen-three
sixteen-twenty-eleven-thirteen
five-eight-eleven-nineteen-six
fourteen-twenty-one-three-two
ninety-twenty-thirty-forty
two-seven-seventy-one-nine
three-thirty-thirteen-zero-one
fourteen-four-forty-five-three
thirteen-thirty-forty-fourteen-four-three

a	f-s-f	l-r-p-v	k-r-o-t-h-c
a-b	k-a-j	v-z-p-m	s-v-b-f-n-q
c-z	p-t-d	u-q-j-a-t	t-l-e-t-i-a-h
t-d	c-g-d	t-z-g-b-v	w-r-x-s-j-i-n

ta-pa	la-du-fa	so-ard-nam-sen
sa-so	sho-nu-snur	fee-lu-say-hi
kee-no	choo-stan-im	ven-log-me-can-fa
fa-rol	pay-ken-mor	im-foo-nab-sith-kal
baw-bu	om-ma-ne-pad	tee-shun-may-by-kip
take-go	me-hum-si-fee	ren-war-miss-lu-pot-fay
feel-sit-da	kye-toe-jim-hop	nam-say-tim-lay-du-lo

Here.
Look there!
I'm hungry
Why not?
Where is she?
Take the train tomorrow.
We'll get off the bus at Albany.
Do you prefer the bus or the train?
When can you come to visit me in Dallas?
There are not too many revolutions in this country.
My sister has three attractive girl friends who like to dance.
Do you see the lady with the brown hat and the two small boys?
John has a top, a knife, two marbles, and a frog in his pocket.

3-d	p-r-n-2	he-ka-no-3-come	d-q-7-fab-3-pan
4-9	8-z-6-L	fee-sam-nun-4-12	9-4-30-c-match-cry
s-2-g	4-ba-t-7	lev-jab-14-my-tak	Please-2-x-h-z-n-h
5-n-x	zen-toe-f-10	6-11-now-throw-bus	8-ban-h-pan-18-10-no
t-4-9-f	1-k-sho-see-r	take-the-11-19-rab	al-t-fu-pye-can-sig-won

By this time, it should be possible to have a fairly definite idea of the student's auditory level and pronunciation patterns, so what next? In a large number of cases, the lacking or low-level abilities will be so noticeable that some teachers will desire to start with them in order to build them up. Others would rather refine the capabilities that are only slightly deviant. Still others will have established a basic pattern of exercises that will be taken by all students regardless of the student's abilities or disabilities. My preference is to work first on what the student states as his most urgent need, and secondly, on what I consider his most urgent need. If both his needs and my conception of his needs may be worked on in the initial period, we should both feel better at the end of the interview.

It is especially important to give the student homework to do during the first session, despite it supposedly being only an initial interview. If possible, teach him a new sound, word, or concept which he may master during the first meeting, even if it is only the correct pronunciation of "hello." The teacher's name is also a good practice item for the first day. It is almost astonishing to note the difficulty that foreign students undergo in trying to learn family and given names. I smilingly tell my students that if they can pronounce my name the first time they try it, they don't need any speech work. One of my former French teachers would gleefully relate the problems French citizens had in pronouncing her name, the last half of which does not exist in French—Smith. A few evenings after my first daughter was born I was teaching a group of orientals from China, Japan and Korea. They were aware of the event and one of the gentlemen politely asked the baby's name. None of them understood me when I spoke it, so I wrote it on the chalk board—Ruth Lee. We spent nearly ten minutes working on the pronunciation.

Another item the student may learn to say is his address. His telephone number may also be difficult for him to pronounce so that Americans might understand it. While taking the case history, the teacher should find several other components of his vital statistics that might be taught him. Before he leaves for the day, the teacher should double-check to be sure that the student knows what he is to practice for the next time, and also that he knows when the next time is. As an extra precaution, it is a good idea to write down the time of the next appointment and the assignment for the student, retaining a carbon copy for the file so that it may be reviewed for the next session.

AFTER THE INITIAL MEETING

At the first session after the initial interview, the teacher will undoubtedly discover that the student wants rules to follow so that he may better learn English. For some reason, foreign students, just as beginning teachers, feel more secure with rules. It doesn't matter that these rules may not be universally and totally true; they are something to cling to during a precarious period of orientation. Memorizing rules and learning some of their simpler applications allows the student to attain a feeling of accomplishment and to "show off" what he has learned to his family and/or friends. In Chapter Two are listed nine basic concepts of teaching CAE pronunciation. The first five of these are convenient to teach the student during the first few sessions. These are explained, exemplified, built upon, combined, reviewed, reviewed, and made the combined basis for most of the training sessions. These rules are:

1. American English is not pronounced as it is spelled;
2. English is not pronounced as it is spaced on paper;
3. The vowels of CAE are usually quite different than the vowels of other languages;
4. When an American sound does not exist in the foreign student's native language, he will substitute for it the most similar sound or sounds of his own language (this provides a rationale for auditory training);
5. It is more important to teach the overall pattern of phrases than it is to teach specific sounds.

Although at times it may be preferable to start with the fifth rule, I habitually take them in the order presented above, explaining them very much as they were explained in Chapter Two while trying to allow leeway for individual differences and needs. The first rule permits the introduction of simple phonetic concepts as they are needed. I do not agree with the linguists who try to teach an entire course in the Phonetics of American English to foreign students prior to teaching them English. The introduction of one or two phonetic symbols in each lesson as a basis for drillwork and homework is sufficient. Symbols should be taught first for the sounds which are most deviant in the student's attempts to pronounce CAE. These most deviant sounds may be either consonants or vowels according to traditional categories. It is difficult at first to decide which of the deviant sounds are *most* deviant, for it is nearly impossible to quantify the amount of deviancy with anything near accuracy. To settle the problem for myself, I have the student read aloud Rule One: *American English is not pronounced as it is spelled.* This is read aloud and tape-recorded first by me, then by the student, again by me and once more by the student. We play back the recording while both of us analyze the differences between his pronunciation, my pronunciation, and what the written sentence would apparently lead to as pronunciations if we had spoken the sentence according to its spelling. His predominant errors are taken as the basis for work to be done. He is taught the phonetic symbols for the sounds he has been substituting and then is taught the phonetic symbols and correct pronunciation for the desired sounds. These are compared and contrasted, drilled on in syllables, words, short phrases and simple sentences. Other incorrect pronunciations are not specifically worked on until some measure of automaticity of self-correction of the first few sounds is evident. However, occasional reference to other errors should be made. One of the strange happenings in this field is that a casual reference to an error other than that being worked on fairly often results in spontaneous correction of that error. I don't know why. It may be that the casual explanation is all that is needed for that particular error. Again, it might be a form of rebellion on the part of the student who may resent having to drill for so long on one or two sounds and decide to do something on his own for spite.

Prolongation, diphthongization, shortening, distortion and disappearance of sounds in context should be taught as part of the pronunciation of the phonemes in their many contexts. For example, $/I/$ as in *him* should not simply be contrasted with $/i/$ as in *he*. The student should be shown that $/I/$ does not sound as loud and clear as $/i/$, that it is often a trifle longer and appears in many people to be slightly more aspirate. When shortened, $/I/$'s pronunciation tends to approximate schwa ($/ə/.$) When $/p/$, $/t/$ and $/k/$ are taught, the difference in the positions within a phrase that will result in altered productions of these consonants should be explained, especially the tendency for Americans to explode these phonemes at the beginning of words in such a way that extra air may be heard in accompaniment with them. The reduction of energy or implosion of $/p/$,

/t/, and /k/ in medial or final phrasal positions should be explained in such a manner that the student realizes that these are not only different pronunciations, but that they also result in a difference of stress patterns within the phrase.

In learning any new psychophysical coordination, there is a possibility that the student will employ too much energy in his attempts. This is true in learning the coordinations for CAE. The articulators will be forced into exaggerated postures, breath may be taken in or released too violently, and there will be heavy stress on the majority of sounds and words, rendering their production monotonous and bizarre. As soon as these symptoms appear, it is time to switch emphasis to the stress pattern, to the "melodic line" of ongoing speech, and to discuss the need for relaxed phonemic production as part of the establishment of a more normal pronunciation. Practice in this area should then be combined with habituation of the correct pronunciation of the phonemes under study. In this wise, a departure may be seen from the tradition of a sound being a sound being a sound. Thus, a reason for drilling on pronunciation of a phoneme in small phrases is to demonstrate that it changes according to the phrase. Let's consider /I/ as in him. In answer to the question, "Do you want to speak to me or to him?" the single-word response is likely to be /hIm/. To "Who wants him?" the answer may be "*I* want /əm/," with /h/ omitted and /I/ changing to schwa because the subject of the sentence received the stress in this instance. If the /h/ had not diminished and if the /I/ had retained its pronunciation the meaning of the phrase might be misconstrued. At best, the pronunciation would seem stilted and artificial.

Consonants as well as vowels alter their characteristics when influenced by neighboring phonemes. In a recent study of how trained judges perceive certain sounds according to their placement between voiced or voiceless sounds, it became apparent that context made a difference in the judges' decisions. A voiced sound before an /s/ tended to cause the /s/ to be produced and perceived more like a /z/. This is not a new finding, and has been known by phoneticians for many years. An accompanying finding is of importance; judges had difficulty agreeing with one another and themselves concerning what they thought they heard normal speakers of American English say. Of thirty-four test groupings of sentences containing /s/, /z/, /f/ and /v/, nearly 12% could be interpreted as *either* /s/ or /z/; 0% were classified as good /s/, /f/, or /v/; 30% were recognizable but not good /s/ or /f/; nearly 53% were recognizable but not good /z/ or /v/; nearly 6% were identified as good /z/. In sum, 94% of the consonants evaluated were not considered well-produced when presented in conversational contexts by three educated speakers of American English—two of whom were speech pathologists (Burkowsky, 1967). These results may be interpreted in a number of fashions. It is easy enough to say that even trained judges cannot listen well. It is more scientific to say that no person pronounces the same sound twice in a row; he may approximate it quite closely, but it is similar rather than identical. Two people will probably not pronounce one sound in the same manner, but again, will produce similar enough acoustic effects so that the meaning will be transmitted to a listener. The results of research along this line are at present causing theorists to lean more toward teaching the sound in a meaningful context as part of a *gestalt* rather than as a separate, unchanging entity. This embraces Rule Two— *English is not pronounced as it is spaced on paper* and Rule Five —*It is more important to teach the overall pattern of phrases than it is to teach specific sounds.* Rule Four—*When an American sound does not exist in the foreign student's native language, he will substitute for it the most similar sound or sounds of his own language*—takes on deeper meaning in terms of the research cited above. If trained judges of American English have difficulty agreeing with themselves and with one another when evaluating speakers of their own language, pity the poor foreign student who has barely a scraping acquaintance with the language!

What are some common phrasal patterns? There are many more than text book writers like to admit. There are monosyllabic utterances which might be considered phrases since they represent complete thoughts. Some of these are:

Yes.	Yes!	Yes?
No.	No!	Nnnno.
Me.	Me!	Me?

Many of these loaded one-word responses should spring readily to mind. Other one-syllable-one-word statements come in the form of greetings, e.g., *Hi!* or commands such as *Look! Don't!*, *etc.* The intonational patterns should be taught for these extremely short vocalizations, but will be more valuable if presented after the student becomes accustomed to practicing on slightly longer phrases.

Short phrases beginning with prepositions, adverbs and conjunctions are more important than they may seem on casual inspection. Prepositions are supposed to help show relationships between parts of a sentence. The relative stress on a preposition may alter the intent of the speaker. Some short phrases which make up a healthy percentage of our speech include:

in the _____	of the _____	below the _____
to the _____	on the _____	between the _____
at the _____	over the _____	beside the _____
by the _____	above the _____	near the _____
for the _____	from the _____	beneath the _____
before the _____	after the _____	about the _____
until the _____	during the _____	with the _____

All of the beginning words indicated may be followed by words other than *the,* but the popularity of phrases wherein a preposition (especially) is followed by *the* and a noun (to the house, at the station, on the way, after the game) make this a frequently heard pattern. The typical foreign student will mispronounce both phonemes of *the,* making any of several substitutions for the /ð/, and a moderately stressed /i/ for the second sound. Our concern is not so much for the /ð/ as it is for the second sound, which may be a number of unstressed phonemes or else /ij/ when the following word begins with a vowel. For the most part, *the* in a prepositional phrase should be unstressed or weakly stressed. The foreign student's inclination to over-stress *the* throws off the melody of the sentence. Therefore, basic prepositions followed by *the* may be preceded and followed by other common words as one means of teaching phrasing, stress, and phoneme production at the same time. Judicious selection of words to accompany the skeletal phrases will build vocabulary. Let us take as our building-block the short combination *in the*:

1. In the house
2. Who's in the house?
3. He's in the house.
4. He's not in the house.
5. He's in the house sleeping.
6. He's in the house every evening.
7. In the house it seems much warmer.
8. Once, in the house, I killed four flies at a time.
9. Once in the house, they hurried to the kitchen.

Now let's add more phrases including *the:*

In the morning, after breakfast and *before the cleaning woman came,* there were, *in the house,* fourteen empty milk cartons waiting to be taken out *to the trash cans near the garage.*

After the student becomes familiar with the concepts and practice of phrase-building he should be encouraged to focus his attention on phrases spoken in other classes, in social conversation, on television or on the radio. Thinking of and listening for phrases will make it easier for him to think and speak in phrases. As part of the training in phrase recognition, oral reading provides a stout crutch. Oral interpretation and voice and diction books contain passages neatly marked according to thought or breath groups. Other formal and informal literature may be treated similarly. Part of each session should then be devoted to conversation structured on phrasal speech. The conversation should be recorded and then analyzed by the teacher and student, followed by correction of pronunciation, grammar, syntax and word choice. Corrected phrases extracted from the conversation are rehearsed until the teacher is satisfied that the student has built up habit patterns that may be easily recalled when needed.

With an individual student, it is much easier to build lessons upon his specific needs than it is with a group. If he is taking other classes, he will need to learn vocabulary specifically for those classes. For this reason, many therapists spend part of each session helping the student learn the terminology of his classes or job. This may go too far though, and the student may look upon the teacher more as a private tutor for passing courses rather than as a teacher of communication.

In this chapter, I have tried to suggest several procedures to be used with individual cases. Each evaluational technique may be modified so that it becomes a teaching tool. In similar fashion, each pedagogical session is part of ongoing diagnosis. Whenever warranted, plans should be altered to insure maximal learning with minimal pain.

CHAPTER XIII

GROUP THERAPY

L ESSONS FOR GROUPS of foreign students require more preparation farther in advance than do those for individual students. There is less opportunity to plan the lessons around specific needs when the combined problems of several students are to be considered. Yet, many of the concepts, tests and exercises suggested for an individual student are applicable to groups as well. It is also still important to have a case history; it is necessary to have an idea of the student's level of English ability and an acute awareness of those linguistic areas in which he is most defective.

With any number of students greater than one it soon becomes obvious that those at different levels are ready for different types of training. If the students demonstrate markedly different capabilities at the time of the initial interview they should be grouped into as many classes as feasible. The number of levels may range from one to as high as six or seven, depending upon the purpose of the program. A beginning teacher or therapist will be more comfortable working with no more than two or possibly three different levels at the most.

Those who fall into the lowest level are easily identified during the first five minutes of the interview. These people often wear a puzzled, sometimes lost look, answer questions poorly if at all, and show tremendous difficulty and numerous errors in phrasing the simplest question. They may have had a year or less of formal training in English in their native countries, or perhaps a short course in a linguistics center immediately after their arrival in this country. They may be thought of as the emergency cases who need as much time as can be given them as often as possible.

Once this group has been established, breaking the others into definite levels is more confusing. A good many teachers and therapists give up in the middle of the decision-making process and decide to maintain only two groups — the aforementioned "emergency" group and the "advanced" group.

Each group should be seen more than once weekly, preferably a minimum of three times. Some teachers who work with foreign students' speech and written language find it convenient to combine the speech groups for one lesson weekly. In this period, they present basic theory and drill which is amplified later in smaller groups or in individual tutoring. My personal preference is to follow this approach, especially if there are a large number of students with the same mother tongue, for if one of the students does not admit that he has failed to understand something, he and his friends will usually talk it over later. From these conversations, the student may eventually attain a proper understanding. Often, his more competent friends will explain to me his specific problems, and through this intermediary technique the process may actually be hastened. This is contrary to what many modern linguists suggest. They would rather that the student be drilled in the repetition of sentences or phrases until the patterns become habitual and effortless. In general, this is a good principal, but unhappily, it doesn't work for all people. For those who understand enough English to realize why they are doing certain types of exercises the repetitious drill works well, but there are others who feel insecure and lost repeating what to them appear strings of mumbo-jumbo. There are still others whose schooling and predispositions have instilled in them a need for thorough knowledge of theory before engaging wholeheartedly in practice. These differences in attitude, if made known early enough, would provide a rationale for regrouping the classes according to the student's desire either for theory, for rapid learning or useful listening and speaking vocabulary, for emphasis on learning to listen well enough to understand classroom teachers or combinations thereof. To me, this orientation makes a great deal of sense, but it is not easy to carry out. As is said in the final chapter of scores of master's theses and doctoral dissertations, "more research is necessary."

If this chapter were aimed at the foreign student whose English-speaking ability is at an advanced level, it would be less difficult for me to be prescriptive with regard to step-by-step-lessons, but such is not the assumption of either this chapter or of the entire book. It is presumed that the reader may be blessed with students whose capacities range from nearly total ignorance of the English language to those who desire just a bit more polish so that they may give the impression of having been born in the United States. Incidentally, several years ago when I was doing private speech therapy and tutoring, the vast majority of foreign accent clients who sought my services were those who wanted to sound like "real Americans."

In the event that there is an advanced, fairly sophisticated group of students, procedures developed by Professor Black and his colleagues at the Ohio State University are worth using. Black's book, *American Speech for Foreign Students* (1963), is intended for just such an elite group. It contains several rules which answer a good many questions that the students may have wondered about, and provides the teacher with a heavily structured series of exercises and drills. If given the opportunity, most students at this level would benefit from having their own copies of the book to use as a text book. An intermediate level student would also derive a certain amount of use from Black's book, but the vocabulary might be too difficult for him. The drills and explanations could be screened by the teacher and employed on a selective basis for both intermediate and low level groups.

BASIC CONCEPTS FOR THE COMBINED GROUPS

Either for one group or for multiple groups, it may be worth combining them one out of each two or three meetings for the presentation of material that is basically necessary to all. The same five basic concepts recommended in the previous chapter for individual cases should be presented here in approximately the same manner as with the individual student, but usually take longer to cover. The difference in time for accomplishing this is due to the need for the teacher to be sure that all of the students understand the concepts before proceeding. With the individual variations among the students in the group, it should take roughly three times as long to achieve communication of the concepts as compared to explaining them to one student. If, however, there are over four students in the group, this is already a saving of time.

To illustrate the first rule: *American English is not pronounced as it is spelled* — I have found it convenient to write the following words on a chalk board:

speak	hose	blood
break	nose	food
freak	dose	good
	lose	
true	goose	mould
sew	choose	could
few		
	comb	done
verse	tomb	gone
horse	bomb	lone
worse		known
	doll	
beard	roll	
heard		
cord	home	
word	some	
cow	pay	
low	say	
shoe	paid	
foe	said	

Then I read aloud a passage from which these words were taken. It was written by Harriet Voxland for the *Minneapolis Star* and reprinted in *Coronet* (February, 1955).

When the English tongue we speak, why is "break" not rhymed with "freak?" Will you tell me why it's true we say "sew" but likewise "few?" And the maker of a verse cannot rhyme his "horse" with "worse?" "Beard" sounds not the same as "heard"; "cord is different from "word"; "cow" is cow, but "low" is low; "shoe" is never rhymed with "foe." Think of "hose" or "nose, then "dose" and "lose"; and think of "goose" and yet of "choose." Think of "comb" and "tomb" and "bomb," "doll" and "roll" and "home" and "some." And since "pay" is rhymed with "say," why not "paid" with "said," I pray? Think of "blood" and "food" and "good"; "mould" is not pronounced like "could." Wherefore "done," but "gone" and "lone"—is there any reason known? To sum up all, it seems to me, sounds and letters don't agree.

As I slowly read this aloud I point to the word which I am going to say next. It is important to point to the word prior to saying it, and to maintain the pointing until the word has been said. After I have read the passage aloud once, I say, "Now I'm going to read it again. Listen carefully to what I say, and look carefully at the words." I then re-read the passage orally, again pointing at the words. After the second reading, I point to the first word, pronounce it, and have the students try it with me three or four times. If the chorus has some sour notes in it or if I suspect that someone is not trying, I have each student try the word, with my assistance, until I am satisfied. I then explain to them that, although the last three letters of "speak" are the same as those of "break," they are pronounced differently, and that there is no one rule to explain it. Not only that, but there are many other words whose written forms look as if they should be pronounced in a certain way, but aren't. We then drill similarly on "break" and "freak," and, in order to increase familiarity with the main pronunciations of *eak*, the phonetic symbols /i/ and /eI/ are introduced. These are written on the board in position over the *ea* in each word. The pronunciations are again practiced, in isolation and then in the words, individually and in chorus. Each word is then put into a short phrase such as "I don't speak English." This phrase is drilled on as if it were one long word. It is written on the board; I say it twice and then with the students do it in chorus. Following this, each student does it individually but with sufficient help to produce it acceptably. Similar procedures are used with all the other words on the list.

In the same fashion, we then work on the second rule: *English is not pronounced as it is spaced on paper.* The sentence is written on the board with connecting loops to bring the words together in such a way that they are treated as parts of a long word:

I don't speak English.

I tell them that this is the way they should think of speaking

English, and that this is the way most Americans speak colloquial American English. To amplify this point I then read the phrase one word at a time in a monotonous voice, after which I say it with normal liaison (linking) and once again with exaggeratedly rapid liaison. The group choruses along with me a few more times at different rates and with emphasis on the rhythm and liaison. Each student has an opportunity to try the phrase two or three or even more times while the other students become judges who vote on whether the phrase sounds reasonably acceptable. After this, each word is put into a question form, and sometimes into an exclamatory form, with similar drills. The students are encouraged to construct oral sentences containing the words and three- or four-sentence short stories employing the word.

Some short sentences usable for lessons based on several words from the original list are presented below. Not all of them are easy to put into short sentences. Note that with each new difficult vowel or consonant that might occur in a word the phonetic symbol may be taught and drilled on. For several class meetings thereafter, the phonetic symbols and their pronunciations should be reviewed, both as auditory training and learning reinforcement.

———————

1. I don't speak English.

   Do you speak English?

   Speak English!

2. You'll break your neck.

   Did you break it?

   Don't break it!

3. That's a true story.

   Is it true?

   That's not true!

4. Please sew my button on.

   Can you sew?

Sew it now!

5. I'll recite a verse for you.

Which verse?

The only verse I know.

6. My horse is lame.

Where's your horse?

Somebody stole my horse!

7. She's feeling worse today.

Is he feeling worse, too?

Things are going from better to worse!

8. A beard makes a face look dirty.

Are you growing a beard?

Look at that beard!

9. I heard a new joke today.

Have you heard this one?

That's the best joke I ever heard!

10. He bought a cord of wood.

Do you have a ball of cord?

This cord is too short.

11. That's the word I was searching for.

What does this word mean?

What an odd word!

12. Cows give us milk.

Have you ever milked a cow?

Holy cow!

13. A low blow is illegal in boxing.

Is the chair too low for you?

It's way too low!

14. A low-heeled shoe is good for working.

Which pair of shoes should I buy?

These shoes hurt my feet!

15. A foe is an enemy.

Is the word *foe* used very much?

No, *foe* is old-fashioned!

16. I use a hose to water the garden.

May I borrow your hose?

There's a run in my new hose (stockings)!

17. My horse won by a nose.

What's that on your nose?

Keep your nose out of other people's business!

18. The doctor gave me a large dose of medicine.

How big was the dose?

It was a gigantic dose!

19. Nobody likes to lose.

How much did you lose?

Don't you dare lose that money!

20. We're having roast goose for dinner.

Is goose too greasy for you?

What a lovely goose!

21. I don't like to have to choose sides.

Who're you going to choose first?

Choose me! Choose me!

22. She wore a comb in her hair.

Will you buy me a new comb?

Ruth, comb your hair!

23. Grant's tomb is in New York City.

Do you want to visit the tomb?

This place is as lively as a tomb!

24. The plane dropped the bomb on the target.

Did the bomb explode?

Look out for the bomb!

25. The doll fell out of the doll carriage.

Does this doll close her eyes?

What a doll!

26. As we rolled along we shared a roll.

Why doesn't this ball roll?

Come on, roll those dice!

Similar sentences may be structured from the remainder of the words on the list. Other words which illustrate specific problems may be introduced in the same fashion. Whenever a student has difficulty with the pronunciation or correct usage of a word or expression in conversation or while otherwise speaking in class, that word or expression may legitimately become part of a lesson.

The fact that a student has attempted to use a word makes it worth studying. The students may be requested to make a list of words that they would like to work over because they have: 1) heard or seen them often without understanding them; 2) wanted to use them but have been unsure of their exact use, or 3) used them and have been laughed at. Upon such a request by the teacher, several words are usually advanced within five minutes, and over half of the students should return with lists for the next class meeting.

In these and other sentences — and it is perfectly permissible to use the same sentence to illustrate other points — it is possible to explain the concepts of rules three and four: *The vowels of CAE are usually quite different than the vowels of other languages* and *When an American sound does not exist in the foreign student's native language, he will substitute for it the most similar sound or sounds of his own language.* As we return to our old friend "I don't speak English," we may recall that we placed linking lines between words to emphasize liaison concepts like this:

I don't speak English.

To demonstrate that English is not pronounced as it is spelled, the phonetic markings may have been placed above certain written letters:

aI
or
ə   i   I   I
I don't speak English.

For the students who confuse /I/ and /i/, the vowels in *speak* and *English* are excellent illustrative examples. When they pronounce these words the teacher should tell them when they are wrong and then produce the vowels contrastively several times, pointing to the phonetic symbol and/or spelling each time. The student is then requested to produce the isolated vowels contrastively upon the demand of the teacher. Usually the /I/ will be pronounced with too much sharpness, tension and loudness; the /i/ will be too short, sharp, and tense. The student will customarily employ one sound for both of these sounds. His sound will be nearer in pronunciation to /i/ than to /I/. Since it is an accepted concept that it is easier to learn a more grossly different pronunciation, it would be considered more logical to teach the differences between the student's substitutive sound and /I/ first. After he has acquired some facility with /I/, it would be theoretically easier to teach differentiations of /I/, the student's substitutive sound, and /i/.

The combination of the final *t* of *don't* and the initial *s* of *speak* are useful in helping Spanish-speaking students to realize that words beginning with *s* do not have an extra syllable. One of the characteristic errors of Spanish speakers is that they tend to prefix such words with an /ɛ/ syllable, thus altering the rhythm. When they are shown that the *t* of *don't* may be thought of as the first sound of *speak,* this permits them to think of the two words either as one long word, or sometimes as *don't speak.* This takes away the vowel they intruded, and while improving the pronunciation of the word *speak,* reduces the phrase by the one extra syllable, bringing the phrasal pattern nearer to the American. This one explanation not only teaches phonetic and liaison concepts; it also illustrates the interaction of these concepts with the fifth rule: *It is more important to teach the overall pattern of phrases than it is to teach specific sounds.*

How may one go about teaching phrasal patterns? Perhaps there is some merit to analyzing typical oral CAE conversations and then setting up formulae for them something like this:

article + *noun* + *verb* + *adjective or adverb* equals one form of simple descriptive phrasal sentence.

This formula may be applied to any of the following sentences:

1. The bus is full.
2. The dog is sick.
3. An elephant is loose.
4. An acrobat was hurt.
5. A girl was crying.
6. A car was damaged.
7. The man fell down.

8. The alarm went off.
9. An eagle dives rapidly.
10. A frog croaked noisily.

In each of the first eight sentences, the second and fourth words might be underlined to indicate that these were the important words within the phrase and should receive stress of one form or another. The article and the verb of each of these sentences are then relatively unstressed. Stress may be manifested by: 1) raising the pitch; 2) lowering the pitch; 3) increasing the intensity; 4) decreasing the intensity; 5) prolonging the vowel; 6) diphthongizing the vowel; 7) pausing before or before and after the word; 8) over-articulating the word, or combinations thereof. The student most commonly elects to use the "punch" method at first, giving a burst of intensity for each stressed word. This should be de-emphasized, and more suitable forms of stress substituted. In these first eight sentences, it may be helpful to think of the article and the noun as a sub-phrasal group connected via liaison with the verb and adjective or adverb. These may be thought of as being akin to (one-half beat plus one full beat) flowing into (one-half beat plus one full beat). Of course, there are additional partial beats in polysyllabic words such as *elephant* in sentence 3, *acrobat* in sentence 4, *crying* in sentence 5, *damaged* in sentence 6, and *alarm* in sentence 8. However, each of these words has *one* relatively stressed syllable.

In sentences nine and ten the stress pattern changes, for although the nouns and adverbs will receive stress, the verbs also contain descriptive qualities. *Croaked* is even onomatopoetic to some degree. A rule of thumb to apply in such instances is: *If a word clarifies or enlivens a phrase, it should be stressed in oral production.* Another general rule is: *Every phrase should have at least one syllable which is moderately or heavily stressed.*

Many teachers think in terms of either three or four levels of stress. In a three-level stress concept one would use:

1. Heavy or strong stress
2. Moderate or medium stress
3. Weak or unstressed

More analytic teachers tend to go to at least four levels:

1. Heavy or strong stress
2. Moderate or medium stress
3. Weak or tertiary stress
4. Unstressed or swallowed

Symbols may be employed in a systematic manner to indicate the type of stress each syllable is to have. It is easiest to place the symbol either above or below the vowel, since stress occurs primarily in the vowel or vowel-like element of a syllable in American English. For unstressed or swallowed syllables, it is more pedagogically dramatic to draw a light line through the letter or letters involved to connote their lack of importance. A line may also be drawn through silent letters. Among the many stress marks I have seen in various systems, the following occur fairly often:

'—preceding the syllable indicates primary, strong, or heavy stress

'—over the vowel indicates strong, or heavy stress

ˌ—preceding the syllable indicates secondary, moderate or medium stress

ˆ—over the vowel indicates secondary, moderate or medium stress

ˋ—over the vowel indicates weak or tertiary stress, and sometimes, unstressed

˘—over the vowel indicates unstressed

In simpler systems, one line under a word may be employed for moderate stress, two lines for heavy stress, and those not underlined are relatively ignored. Some teachers, especially teachers of the deaf or the brain-injured, may prefer to color-code their underlinings, using a different color for each degree of stress. Once again, it doesn't matter which code is used as long as it is used consistently.

Following the analytic pattern as exemplified by the ten practice sentences above, it is possible to set up a series of formulae for other phrasal and sentence patterns. For those who care to do so, it is perhaps most efficient to consult texts written by those who have a *structuralist* orientation to teaching English grammar and composition. Such texts should contain not only the formulae, but also illustrative phrases and sentences. Too often, however, these sentences are artificial or contain obsolete terminology.

My preference is to do as little of this as possible, for I do not believe that *all* of oral language can be analyzed and formularised efficiently and quickly for practical pedagogical purposes. Direct imitation is probably more efficient and rapid than any other technique, regardless of the length and complexity of sentence and phrasal structures. But, direct imitation must be coupled with explanations and illustrations fairly often during the session so that comprehension accompanies acquisition of skills.

CATEGORIES

With groups of students, the use of *categories* presents a type of structure while still allowing a great deal of leeway for timely or impromptu tangents to be followed. As is so often the case in academic classrooms, the tangents may prove eventually to be more valuable than the carefully pre-planned material. At the Sorbonne, the category approach has been used quite effectively in the teaching of French vocabulary to French teachers from foreign countries. The technique involves choosing a topic for the day and compiling a list of words, phrases or expressions commonly associated with the topic. The pronunciations are rehearsed, after which the students attempt to construct sentences based on them. Following this, the teacher may ask questions of a student concerning the topic. The student answers the teacher and may then ask the teacher a question. For variety, the student may ask a question of another student who in turn answers and then asks another student, setting up a chain of short dialogues. If time remains in the period, all or selected students may give short speeches on the category as related to their native countries or personal interests and experiences. Often, the category can be carried over to a subsequent meeting, the students being assigned to collect more terminology and information during the interval between sessions. This additional terminology is then pooled, shared, and integrated with the previous material.

Topics for category exercises may be of local or global interest. Where all or the majority of the students are new to the specific geographic area the first category lesson may be enlivened with a city, regional, or even campus map.

A more global category would be *transportation*. A nucleus for this topic would include both general and specific terms. By itself, a word might imply a number of meanings, so it becomes necessary to teach the various differences in phrasing that accompany such words. *Ride,* for instance, takes many forms:

ride, take a ride, go for a ride, go riding, ride a bike,
ride a horse, ride a bus, ride *on* a train, ride *in* a car,
ride *in* an airplane, ride slowly, ride rapidly, ride as fast as possible,
ride away, etc.

Then there are the grammatic aspects of:

I ride; I do ride; I am riding;
You ride; you do ride; you are riding:
He or she rides; he or she does ride; he or she is riding;
We ride; we do ride; we are riding;
They ride; they do ride; they are riding.

— and these present tense manifestations also have contracted pronunciations such as *I'm riding, you're riding, he's riding, she's riding, we're riding* and *they're riding.* Thus the root word must be learned not only as a vocabulary term but in its grammatical and syntactic environments so that automaticity of correct usage results. It is therefore quite legitimate to practice the root term in the various past, future and other common tenses as part of the drill within the category. For example, the teacher may drill on the pronunciation of *ride* and then ask a student: "When you came to Syracuse, did you ride here in an airplane?" the teacher should have him learn and drill on at least one of the correct responses.

Complex grammatical structures such as "I would like to have ridden here in an airplane" are often attempted by sophisticated or slightly sophisticated students in conversational practice once they become accustomed to the opportunity for trying new and different patterns that goes along with using a category approach. The teacher may select illustrative phrases, sentences, paragraphs and stories for each category. This illustrative material can be as diverse, informational and colorful as the teacher prefers. One teacher may employ emotionally sterile phrases and contrived passages; another may extract pertinent material from his own experience; a third may try to base his illustrative material on the student's presumed experience; a fourth may use a standardized lesson plan written by a textbook author or by a master teacher; a fifth may seek dramatic examples intended to shock the student into remembering the concept; a sixth may use mnemonic devices of a logical associative nature. Several combinations of the foregoing techniques are possible in addition to such things as: 1) showing a picture representing the category and having the students and/or the teacher use the picture as a basis for developing terminology, or 2) listening to a recording or a radio or television discussion related to the category as a basis for discovering words and expressions used by the speakers.

To continue with the category of *transportation*, let us contemplate the wealth of vocabulary and culture that the following words may conjure: buggy, carriage, car, limousine, hack, horse, thoroughbred, nag, truck, diesel, monorail, jet, stratocruiser, shank's mare, submarine, cruiser, yacht, canoe, rowboat, balloon, dirigible, dromedary, yak, Jonah, stage coach, clipper ship, sampan, raft, steamer, gondola, chariot, papoose. Any one of these words might become the basis of an entire lesson, if so desired. Take the word *car* as an example. One could discuss the types and brand names of cars currently and previously fashionable in this and other countries, state and national rules for minimum manufacturing requirements, driving regulations, where locally to purchase cars and to procure licenses, how to drive a car, the route one takes each day between home and work, the cost of maintaining a car, difficulty in finding convenient parking, side trips that one may make by car within specified time limits, the problems one has in finding a good mechanic to service a car, antique autos, local lovers' lanes, difficulty of adapting to different transmission systems, how often to have the car serviced in this climate, the efficacy of tank or head-bolt heaters in cold climates, and the rising death rate.

It doesn't matter what category or sub-categorical term is stressed. When the student group is ready to deal with questions, answers, and discussion situations, the category approach serves more as a semblance of structure within which much flexibility is possible than it does to dictate a closely structured session. Yet, in earlier stages of development it can easily provide a highly structured type of situation. As an example, let us take the category or topic: *The average day of a student.*

In this close-knit approach, the group drills on phrases and sentences which deal with the daily schedules and tribulations of either an American student, a foreign student or both. To present contrastive living patterns it is even conceivable to pair an American student with a foreign student as room mates in this saga. The American student, if possible, should be given a name that is difficult for most foreign students to pronounce, and the foreign student's name should be capable of anglicization so that the group may better comprehend the utility of using an American-type name to substitute for their own when dealing with Americans who would give up trying to pronounce their names otherwise. In this example, the room mates are Bruce Westinghouse from Denver, Colorado, and Petrushi Gesundheit from Snitzletonia. Denver exists, but Snitzletonia obviously doesn't which allows us to make it a small but ancient principality with much indifference to modern concepts while at the same time maintaining its own time-honored customs and laws. In Snitzletonia, for instance, there may be no electricity, so its inhabitants still go to bed early and rise early, which could lead to a difference in Bruce's and Petrushi's sleeping and study habits. Raw onions and garlic might be standard food for Petrushi but seldom if ever eaten by Bruce, while in Snitzletonia a male would be considered effeminate and immoral if he used after-shave lotion or hair tonic.

This is not an exaggerated situation. One of my former Thai students was so accustomed to garlic that he carried garlic powder in his pocket to add to student restaurant food. His room mate insisted that he brush his teeth immediately upon entering the room, and continually flung the windows open after he had been in the room for awhile. Conversely, the Thai student would become violently ill when eating certain types of American food, especially rice when prepared in the student restaurant. This approach to depicting an idealized daily schedule will be of interest to many of the students in the group, for if they have American room mates they may feel better when they see similarities between their room mate and Petrushi's, and if they do not live with Americans they may gain insight into some typical American behavior.

Into this structure may be placed study and dating techniques, and indication of the extent and forms of extra-curricular activities, hints on how to stretch money, procedures and terminology for accomplishing the activities of daily life. Eventually, Petrushi may be invited to visit Bruce's family. This would permit further use of terms relating to transportation, family life and leisurely social activities. While the story unfolds, each sentence may be drilled on and elucidated. Questions by the students may be answered by the teacher, who should willingly go off on tangents to thoroughly explain the concepts within each phrase when necessary. Here is the beginning of such a story:

1. Bruce Westinghouse lives in a dormitory.
2. He has a room mate.
3. His room mate's name is Petrushi Gesundheit.
4. Bruce's parents live in Denver, Colorado.
5. Petrushi's parents live in Snitzletonia.
6. Petrushi couldn't pronounce Bruce's name.
7. Bruce couldn't pronounce Petrushi's name either, so he called him Pete.
8. After awhile Petrushi could almost pronounce Bruce's name correctly.
9. Bruce is attending the University on a scholarship.
10. Pete's family is paying for his education.
11. At first, Bruce and Pete didn't get along very well.
12. Their habits were quite different.
13. Pete went to bed as soon as it got dark.
14. Bruce stayed up til the wee hours of the morning.
15. When Pete got up at daybreak, it disturbed Bruce.

16. Bruce liked the windows open, but Pete preferred them closed.

17. Bruce studied while listening to music.

18. Pete was used to studying in a quiet room.

19. Bruce was boisterous, but Pete was the silent type.

20. Pete thought that Bruce led a spoiled, luxurious life.

21. Bruce thought that Pete was a naive, penny-pinching kid.

22. Pete was shocked that Bruce wasted money on records, magazines, movies and girls.

23. Bruce felt ashamed of his room mate who didn't know about American sports or popular music.

24. Every morning Pete woke up first.

25. He washed, shaved and dressed, and then awakened Bruce.

26. Bruce would get up slowly, rubbing his eyes.

27. While Bruce was in the bathroom Pete would study some more.

28. After Bruce had dressed, the boys left for breakfast.

29. They ate in the student cafeteria.

30. Bruce usually ate cereal, eggs, ham or bacon, toast and milk.

31. Pete would have a roll and butter with either coffee or hot chocolate.

32. The food wasn't especially good, but it was filling.

These thirty-two sentences when drilled and discussed in detail could easily and profitably fill two clock hours of class. The story could be continued either as one part of each class or as the basis for the entire class for several class meetings. If begun on a low-enough level, it might provide the skeleton for the entire training program with a given group. If pictures could be used to represent most of the sequence of the story, the emphasis could be primarily on the oral and auditory aspect of language training. If, however, written sentences were used without pictures, it would probably take longer to demonstrate the desired ideas, pictures being more readily understood than verbal explanations.

OTHER GROUP ACTIVITIES

What other methods or techniques are practical for groups? How may the teacher take advantage of his own capabilities and interests to further the abilities of his students?

The teacher's musical abilities, slight though they may be, should be sufficient for him to beat out a stress pattern. This may be done with a drum, by foot tapping, by waving his hand or a baton as a conductor would lead an orchestra, by pounding on a desk or table, by nodding his head vigorously, or by vocally producing melodic noises for the students to follow in a choric fashion.

Contrary to the usual pattern of European languages in which the heavily stressed sound is commonly the last syllable in the word, American English words very often (but not always) receive stress toward the beginning or middle of the word. It is not exactly known why this difference should be so, but some guesses may be made. The european languages which developed from and combined with Latin kept many of the Latin words but shortened most of the long ones. The penultimate (next to the last) syllable in many Latin words usually received stress. When these words were shortened, the last syllables were apparently less important for comprehension and so disappeared as the barbarians of the time modified Latin to their needs. For this possible reason, the last of the syllables to be retained maintain the stress in the derivative Latin languages of today. As American English developed from a combination of several languages over a relatively short time perhaps it was felt that, in many cases, the first part of certain words was most important to its recognition and should receive the stress. (It may be noted that many of our less educated Americans tend to put their stress further forward in words than do many of the better educated Americans.) Possibly this may have been one reason for moving the stress forward. Another potential factor is that during pioneer days when much physical work needed to be done, there was less opportunity for talk during the day and the fatigued laborer did not have sufficient energy or company for practicing lilting conversation (the monosyllabic farmer and plainsman have been immortalized in American literature). Perhaps it was a symptom of the early American filial negation of european styles and influences compounded with piety which influenced them toward the simpler language of the King James version of the Bible. Whatever the reason, CAE stress patterns are often begun with a burst of energy which dies down and then builds up a number of times commensurate with the length of the utterance and then fades toward the end of the phrase or sentence. If we were to add to this our tendency to stretch certain sounds and swallow others, we would notice that our melodic patterns in many instances resemble diminished sine waves:

while many European languages impress us as being more staccato and vigorous to the last syllable:

and oriental, semitic and African languages contain several melodic patterns whose cadences and extra frictional or plosive components sound odd to our unsophisticated ears.

The teacher should listen to his own speech as he pronounces phrases, exaggerate the melodic pattern (a combination of stress, pitch and time) and then select his method of demonstrating the "beat" to his students in as dramatic a manner as he can.

CHORAL READING

Closely allied to music is choral reading — the reading aloud of a text by a group under the direction of a leader. As the teacher reads or speaks the phrases, the students are expected to keep in time with him and with each other. The teacher faces the group so that his voice is channelled more directly toward their ears than are the voices of their classmates. Also, the security and confidence of the teacher lend additional strength and clarity to his voice. At first, the students will speak softly in order not to be overheard if they should err, and learn to focus upon predicting the melodic pattern they are to follow. Once the melody approximates the model, their voices grow stronger and they may concentrate upon the more noticeable articulatory deviations. Often, the adjustments that are made to elicit the correct melody will force a modification of the articulation and facilitate articulation training. The ritualistic repetition of memorized passages helps to build a group feeling and individual self-confidence.

Passages for choral reading should be chosen with care. They should be conversational in tone, and preferably contain built-in requirements of vocal variety.

ROLE PLAYING

One method of assuring that there will be vocal variety inherent in material to be read aloud is to load it with more than one character's speech. The simplest way of doing this is to choose a narration which has somewhere within it a quotation as:

Three men were walking toward the beach when, all of a sudden, one of them stopped to tie his shoe laces. The other two kept on walking. The man who was left behind shouted "Hey! Wait for me!"

In this passage, simple narration was contrasted sharply with a shout, adhering to the concept that it is best to start the teaching of fine difference by working with gross differences. After the students are capable of performing this chore with some degree of adequacy, two and then three characters with different personalities may be encompassed in each exercise, until, eventually, the students may even perform a short scene from a play, portraying several roles. When they become more sophisticated, the students may be told to pretend that they are specific imaginary characters in a given situation and develop an impromptu conversation. This is quite challenging to the majority of students and should not be introduced too early in their training.

SPEECH AND LANGUAGE GAMES

Competition may be brought into the lessons after the students demonstrate that they feel comfortable in the learning environment. To sharpen their minds and stretch their abilities, the teacher may begin a phrase, ask one student to complete it, have a second student supply an additional phrase which amplifies and modifies the previous one, and continue this until the sentence is incapable of further acceptable modification. The teacher might start out with "Once upon . . ." and point to a student who adds "a time . . ." and in turn points to another student who says "many years ago . . ." and chooses a third student and so on. A student who cannot continue "loses," and must start a new chain.

A variant of this consists of having the teacher say a short sentence and point to a member of the class who must begin a new sentence with the last word of the previous sentence. This, too, continues until the players are "stumped."

Another game is *Impressions*, in which the goal is for whoever is "it" to display the speech and mannerisms of either a well-known personality or a member of the class. The students must guess his identity in complete interrogative sentences. The answers are to be given in complete sentences. For example:

"Are you Gary Cooper?" "No, I'm not Gary Cooper."

Trip me up or *Catch my mistake* is another popular game which can be played on several levels. The teacher or student deliberately makes a mistake in pronunciation, grammar or meaning. The class member who first catches the mistake indicates the error and attempts to produce the word, phrase or sentence correctly. The other students judge the correctness of his attempt and may either accept or reject it. If there is insufficient participation in this game, or if a few students prove particularly superior or aggressive, the teacher may insist upon each student taking a turn at being the judge or "it." Forced participation of this nature produces somewhat inhibited and reluctant initial cooperation, but gradually results in more active and aggressive behavior.

Arithmetic problems may be worked on orally and visually as a means of introducing American terms and techniques. After mathematical terminology has been introduced, it may be vitalized and habituated by breaking the class into teams and by having them compete to see which team can solve the greatest number of problems while using correct grammar and pronunciation. This may be in an equivalent form to the old-time "spelling-bee" where the players who responded incorrectly sat down or were eliminated. However, this would not be good for the foreign students with lower abilities who would be discouraged (or even secretly glad) if eliminated on the first trial. Therefore, it would be preferable to keep score of correct and incorrect responses over three attempts to respond to the question, with a decreasing number of points for each successive attempt. Thus, if the first attempt were correct the contestant would receive three points, on the second attempt two points, on the third one point, and if entirely unsuccessful even with aid — no points. The additional trials provide a built-in opportunity for the teacher to give relatively more time and aid to the student who has most need of it. This technique may be applied to other topical areas with varying degrees of success, and should enable the teacher to tap the abilities and academic areas of interest of all of the students.

EPILOGUE:
TERMINATION OF TRAINING

THERE ARE AT LEAST seven reasons for the termination of training:

1. The student leaves the school or geographical area, perhaps to return to his native country;
2. He achieves such a level of competance that he no longer requires or desires the specialized instruction;
3. He can no longer afford the time since he has committments to achieve several other competancies or to accomplish other specific tasks;
4. He becomes physically or emotionally incapable of maintaining his status;
5. The student and teacher may or may not wish to work together for any of a number of reasons;
6. The instruction may be based on a school year or semester calendar, with no allowance for needs that go beyond the calendar;
7. The teacher may change or terminate employment, or, in the case of student teachers or clinicians, it may be time to either switch to another pedagogical experience or to graduate from college.

Whatever the reason, it is hoped that the student feels that the experience has been meaningful and supportive. The teacher, whether novice or experienced, should have learned something new from the student. If the teacher has learned nothing new, there is something wrong with the teacher, for a good teacher ceases to be a good teacher when he is incapable of learning from his students.

SELECTED REFERENCES

ALCORN, K.: Speech development through vibration. *Volta Review, 40*:633-638, 1938.

ALCORN, S.: Development of speech by the Tadoma Method. *Proceedings of the 32nd Convention of American Instructors of the Deaf.* U. S. Government Printing Office, Washington 1941.

BLACK, J., SINGH, S., TOSI, O., TAKEFUTA, Y., and JANCOSEK, E.: Speech and aural comprehension of foreign students. *Journal of Speech and Hearing Research, 8*:43-48, 1965.

BLOCH, BERNARD, and TRAGER, GEORGE L.: *Outline of Linguistic Analysis.* Baltimore, Linguistic Society of America, 1942.

BRONSTEIN, A.: *The Pronunciation of American English.* New York, Appleton-Century-Crofts, 1960.

BRONSTEIN, A.: Some unresolved phonetic-phonemic symbolization problems. *Quarterly Journal of Speech, XLVII*:54-59, 1961.

BRONSTEIN, A., and RAMBO, D.: Language analysis and the speech Teacher —A new frontier. *The Speech Teacher, XI*:130-135, 1962.

BURKOWSKY, M.: A study of the perception of adjacent fricative consonants. *Phonetica, 17*:38-45, 1967.

CARR, E. B.: Teaching *th* sounds of English. *TESOL*, 1, *1*:7-14, 1967.

CARTIER, F. A.: Some important oddities of English phonetics. *TESOL*, 1, *3*: 52-55, 1967.

CROFT, K.: Some co-occurances in American clichés. *TESOL*, v, *2*:47-49, 1967.

DIEHL, C., WHITE, R., and BURK, K.: Rate and communication. *Speech Monographs, XXVI*:229-232, 1959.

DIEHL, C., WHITE, R., and SATZ, P.: Pitch change and comprehension. *Speech Monographs, XXVII*:65-69, 1961.

FAIRBANKS, G.: *Voice and Articulation Drillbook.* New York, Harper, 1960.

FRANCIS, W.: *The Structure of American English.* Ronald, New York, 1958.

GLEASON, H. A., JR.: *An Introduction to Descriptive Linguistics.* Holt, New York, 1955.

IRWIN, R.: A problem of assimilation. *Quarterly Journal of Speech, XLVI*: 302-303, 1960.

IVES, S.: Work paper for Texas Conference on Linguistics, "Phonemics of American English." Unpublished, 1956.

JANN, G., WARD, M., and JANN, H.: A longitudinal study of articulation, deglutition and malocclusion. *Journal of Speech and Hearing Disorders, 29*:424-435, 1964.

JUDSON, L., and WEAVER, A.: *Voice Science*. New York, Appleton-Century-Crofts, 1965.

KENYON, J. S., and KNOTT, T. A.: *A Pronouncing Dictionary of American English*. Springfield, Mass., Merriam, 1949.

LADO, R.: Linguistic interpretation of speech problems of foreign students. *Quarterly Journal of Speech, XLVI*:171-175, 1960.

LARUDEE, F.: Teaching short serial items in a target language. *TESOL,* 1, 2:55-57, 1967.

LLOYD, and WARFEL: *American English in its Cultural Setting*. New York, Knopf, 1956.

LOGAN, H. L.: *Coral Way: A bilingual school. TESOL, 1,* 2:50-54, 1967.

MACDONALD, E.: *Articulation Testing and Treatment: A Sensory-motor Approach*. Pittsburgh, Stanwix House, 1964.

MACPHERSON, R.: *Tongue Tip Patterns of Movement and Shape in Normal Speaking*. Ph.D. Dissertation, Syracuse University, 1968.

MAYER, E.: *Guide to Pronunciation*. Detroit, Wayne State University Bookstore, 1958.

MOSES, E. M.: *Phonetics*. Englewood Cliffs, N. J., Prentice-Hall, 1964.

NEMOY, E., and DAVIS, S.: *The Correction of Defective Consonant Sounds*. Magnolia, Mass., The Expression Company, 1948.

NEWMARK, L., MINTZ, J., and HINELY, J.: *Using American English,* New York, Harper & Row, 1964.

NICHOLS, A.: Apparent factors leading to errors in audition made by foreign students. *Speech Monographs, XXXI*:85-91, 1964.

OWEN, G. H.: *The Sound System of English*. Unpublished paper delivered before the Linguistic Society of Metropolitan Detroit, April, 1961.

PICKLER, J., and LEUTENEGGER, R.: The prediction of phonetic transcription ability. *Speech Monographs, XXIX*:288-297, 1962.

POTTER, R., KOPP, G., and GREEN, H.: *Visible Speech*. New York, D. Van Nostrand, 1947.

PRATOR, C.: *Manual of American English Pronunciation*. New York, Rinehart, 1957.

ROBINETT, B. W. (Ed.) : *On Teaching English to Speakers of Other Languages*. Institute of Language and Linguistics, Georgetown University, Washington, D.C., 1967. See especially articles by G. S. Nutley, R. B. Long, A. Macleish, C. J. Kriedler, and R. S. Schwartz.

SCHUELER, H.: Audio-lingual aids to language training—Aids and limitations. *Quarterly Journal of Speech, XLVII*:288-292, 1961.

SMITH, HENRY LEE: *Linguistic Science and the Teaching of English*. Cambridge, Harvard U. Press, 1956.

STEVENS, C., BRONSTEIN, A., and WONG, H.: English as a second language—Practices of speech departments. *Quarterly Journal of Speech, XLVIII*: 285-290, 1962.

SUTHERLAND, K. K.: The place of dictation in the language classroom. *TESOL, 1, 1*:24-29, 1967.

TRAGER, GEORGE, L.: "Linguistics," signed article in the *Encyclopaedia Britannica,* 1956 edition, volume 14, pp. 162A-162H.

TRAGER, GEORGE L.: *Phonetics: Glossary and Tables.* Buffalo, Studies in Linguistics. Occasional Paper #6, 1958.

TRAGER, GEORGE L., and BLOCH, BERNARD: The syllabic phonemes of english. *Language, 17:*223-46, 1941.

TRAGER, GEORGE L., and SMITH, HENRY LEE: *An Outline of English Structure.* Studies in Linguistics. Occasional Paper #3, 1951, revised 1956.

WISE, C.: Some English problem sounds for Cantonese students. *The Speech Teacher, XII:*92-104, 1963.

YOUNG, E., and HAWK, S.: *Moto-Kinesthetic Speech Training.* Palo Alto, Stanford University Press, 1955.

APPENDIX A
SPEECH TEXTS TO BE USED AS SOURCES

AKIN, J.:*And So We Speak*. Englewood Cliffs, N. J., Prentice-Hall, 1958. This gives a simple introduction to the production of spoken American English.

BRIGANCE, W., and HENDERSON, F.: *A-Drill Manual for Improving Speech*, 2nd ed. Chicago, Lippincott, 1945. This book is important in that it was written by speech and speech correction teachers who worked extensively with speech of foreign students.

BRONSTEIN, A.: *The Pronunciation of American English*. New York, Appleton-Century-Crofts, 1960. This provides an introduction to modern phonetics and language usage, and offers a rationale for understanding the continuous alteration of the English language. It is easy to read and makes a good deal of sense, but tends to emphasize pronunciations of Northeastern United States.

BRONSTEIN, A., and JACOBY, B.: *Your Speech and Voice*. New York, Random House, 1967. While useful as an introductory text to phonetic, phonemic and linguistic theory, it also incorporates recent scientific findings and practice material.

BYRNE, M.: *The Child Speaks*. New York, Harper and Row, 1965. For those who wish to understand one orientation toward auditory and articulatory training for young children, this presents a detailed, easily comprehended procedure. It is to a great extent patterned on Nemoy and Davis: *The Correction of Defective Consonant Sounds*, (1948) but is not intended to be as versatile as the 1948 text.

CARRELL, J., and TIFFANY, W.: *Phonetics*. New York, McGraw-Hill, 1960. A medium-high level phonetic text despite the authors' stated hope that a student could use the book by himself. This book may be read and understood on many levels according to the sophistication of the reader.

107

CLARK, S. H.: *Interpretation of the Printed Page*. Chicago, Row, Peterson and Company, 1915. Primarily of historical interest, this is considered the first of the modern Oral Interpretation texts. If it is available, read it for the methodology concerning phrasing and intonation!

EISENSON, J.: *The Improvement of Voice and Diction*, 2nd ed. New York, MacMillan, 1965. A low to medium level text which introduces phonetic concepts and their application to speech improvement. Several helpful exercises are included.

FISHER, H.: *Improving Voice and Articulation*. Boston, Houghton Mifflin, 1966. There is a speech correction slant to this book, with numerous applications to individual and group speech improvement. Much information from many fields is presented.

FULTON, R., and TRUEBLOOD, T.: *Practical Elements of Elocution*, Boston, Ginn and Company, 1894. Despite its age this is one of the more thoroughly modern texts in this list. At one time it was employed extensively in a variety of courses. Its influence may be observed in the majority of drillbooks, voice and diction and speech correction texts of the twentieth century. If it should be available, read it for fun!

GORDON, M., and WONG, H.:*A Manual for Speech Improvement*. Englewood Cliffs, N.J., Prentice-Hall, 1961. This book is aimed at bilingual speakers of English and at foreign students —especially those whose languages are found in Hawaii and Southeast Asia. A foreign student with some sophistication in reading English might also use this as a text.

HANLEY, T., and THURMAN, W.: *Developing Vocal Skills*. New York, Rinehart and Winston, 1962. A multi-level book which provides an introduction to acoustics, phonetics, speech therapy and psycholinguistic theory. This is more for the slightly sophisticated reader than for the neophyte.

HIBBIT, G., and NORMAN, R.: *Guide to Speech Training*. New York, Ronald Press, 1964. This may be used as a source of exercise and practice material. Care should be taken to avoid many of the overly-formal and classical literary passages which bear little resemblance to modern spoken English.

IRWIN, R. B.: *Speech and Hearing Therapy*. Pittsburgh, Stanwix House, 1965. For those who desire a healthy orientation to speech problems in elementary and high schools, this is one of the more practical and better-written books available. It is excellent for naive readers and quite meaningful for more experienced practitioners.

JOHNSON, W., BROWN, S., CURTIS, J., EDNEY, C., and KEASTER, J.: *Speech Handicapped School Children*, 3rd ed. New York, Harper and Row, 1967. A survey of the field of Speech Pathology with special emphasis upon children.

KING, R., and DIMICHAEL, E.: *Improving Articulation and Voice* New York, MacMillan, 1966. This is a multi-purpose speech text which espouses a dynamic approach to speech training. It is not difficult to read. Many useful ideas may be gleaned from this source.

KOPP, H.: *Some Functional Applications of Basic Phonetic Principals*. Ann Arbor, The Edwards Letter Shop, 1948. There are 56 pages in this very short book which tries to live up to its title, is easily understood and used by an unsophisticated reader.

LIEBERMAN, P.: *Intonation, Perception, and Language*. Cambridge, Massachusetts, M.I.T. Press. 1967. A research-oriented work building on the theory of the *breath-group*, this is for the extremely sophisticated reader who understands the implications of spectral analysis of speech sounds and who can follow the mathematical formulae which Lieberman employs to explain his own and other theorists' working concepts.

MOSES, E.: *Phonetics*. Englewood Cliffs, N. J., Prentice-Hall, 1964. This is a rather high-level book dealing with the history and multiple uses of Phonetics. It should be read after the contents of introductory texts have been mastered.

THOMAS, C.: *The Phonetics of American English*, 2nd ed. New York, The Ronald Press, 1958. This is a not-too-sophisticated introductory text which has been used fairly widely for basic courses in Phonetics. Some of the concepts are inaccurate in terms of recent scientific findings, but the author writes in a fashion which helps the reader feel more confident in the mastery of the subject matter.

VAN RIPER, C.: *Speech Correction,* 4th ed. Englewood Cliffs, N.J., Prentice-Hall, 1963. Van Riper includes both basic and advanced concepts which encompass the entire field of speech pathology in such a manner that the beginning student feels that it is a thorough introductory text while the advanced student who re-reads it is almost startled at the subtle implications which were unnoticed during previous readings.

WISE, C.: *Introduction to Phonetics.* Englewood Cliffs, N. J., Prentice-Hall, 1958. Although an introductory text, this is of a rather scholarly nature. It was extracted from the same author's more complete 1957 volume, *Applied Phonetics.*

APPENDIX B
SUMMARY OF A GROUP PROGRAM

By

MAUREEN MORAN, M.A.

Our class met for the first time in February of 1968. One would be hard pressed to find a more disparate group. There were three Czechoslovakian professors, graduate students from Taiwan, Korea, Japan and Colombia and a Greek Priest. Their English language background was as diversified as their nationalities and careers. There was one uniting force, however, regardless of how many years they had studied English: they were all deficient in pronunciation and aural comprehension.

There were many problems with which to contend. For many this was their first encounter with a young woman teacher. My authority was put to the test during our first meeting. After some verbal dueling in which my position as a language specialist and a native born speaker was asserted, this situation was resolved.

The next problem required a bit more "psychology", for it dealt with how the students presented themselves. Pride is a fine thing but it can become very inhibitory in a classroom. All my students were most reticent to expose their deficiencies — and without a willingness to make mistakes, correction is almost impossible. The need to create a benign environment in any therapy situation is well known. It requires much honesty and acceptance on the part of the therapist. The building of trust is a delicate operation. However, once constructed one is limited only by those approaches which work. Any thing, device or gimmick, that works can and should be used. To that end the therapist becomes at once jester, cajoler, mother-confessor, mimic, cheerleader, and coach.

111

The students were presented with these basic concepts of American English pronunciation:

1. American English is sloppy.
2. American English is not pronounced as spelled.
3. American English is not said as spaced on paper.

These three tenets could not be over-stressed. In the confusion of our language there was some security in knowing what *not* to do. This need for "definiteness" and security was somewhat alleviated by the incorporation of certain codes and stress rules.

The International Phonetic Alphabet was taught to my students. In terms of articulation, one prime concern was with vowels and certain consonants (/r/, /l/, /s/, /tsh/, /s/). I was surprised to discover the similarity of articulation errors in a group of such diverse national backgrounds. Be they Czech, Chinese or Greek, they all distorted the American /r/! Working with phonetic symbols added a visual aid to the auditory correction. Fairbank's rules of stress and intonation were later taught. They served as guide-posts in murky territory. There are few rules which have realistic application to American English pronunciation. The therapist is obligated to offer the student what she can.

The bulk of our work was directed toward auditory training ("developing the American ear") and drill on American stress and intonation. The importance of the latter was demonstrated to my class when I spoke a phrase in each of their languages with exaggerated American intonation. The class agreed that the words were right, but understanding was sacrificed by incorrect intonation. As in all therapy, repetition and practice are essential to change. Drill passages were selected in terms of meaningfulness to the student. Frequently I would compose a story which dealt with campus news or current events. The story was placed on the blackboard with diacritical markings for stress. Then through imitation and repeated trials the intonation was learned.

Auditory training was developed, again, through drill. I discovered that techniques used in Aphasia therapy had application to foreign accent work.

One cannot adequately teach the language without teaching something of the culture. In each session, there was time set aside for questions about American culture as well as language. These times were important not only for information gathering but for speech practice as well.

Toward the end of the semester we began devoting more time to spontaneous exchange. Therapy activities such as role-playing (restaurant; shopping for clothes; library) and a conversational approach were used. The students were surprisingly free and good-natured about these sessions. There was always a lively exchange with well-meaning criticism, joking, and correction a part of the lesson.

Evaluation is a difficult proposition. Having been so dynamically involved tends to cloud one's objectivity. It was here that my test was of importance for it allowed accurate subjective evaluation. *My students left class at the end of the semester needing additional work on specific sound pronunciation. But they also left with a greatly improved auditory comprehension level and a greatly increased willingness to speak. Neither gain was a minor acquisition. I'm confident that with additional speaking practice quite adequate American pronunciation will develop.

---

*See Appendix C.

APPENDIX C
MORAN SURVEY OF ENGLISH USAGE

T HE MORAN SURVEY of English usage is intended as a quick means of assessing the language ability of non-native English language speakers. The survey is devised with particular reference to the foreign student population in attendance at most American colleges and universities. The test items dealing with Dictation and Oral Comprehension reflect our awareness of this population. The language of both items is on a college reading level. The students come here with an English language background which is almost exclusively visual. Therefore, we anticipate a modicum of success when they are dealing with this modality.

The section on Echoic Response is of particular interest to the language therapist. It assesses at once articulation and imitative ability. Receptivity to imitation is usually a good prognostic sign.

The items included under Contextual Phonemic Discrimination are designed to test both phonologic ability and auditory discrimination. The importance of drill work on auditory processes cannot be over emphasized. Foreign accent work, like any language therapy, requires a strong foundation of auditory ability. Training in the "American Ear" is half the work of Foreign accent therapy.

The foreign student will probably make predictable errors on all items tested. The written sections will produce spelling errors as well as occasional word omissions. These areas, however, will be the areas of greatest success. Contextual Phonemic Discrimination will produce a depressed score. Contrasting phonemes presented aurally offer many problems to those who are visually oriented. The items dealing with Echoic Response and Reading Discrimination will reveal many articulation errors. These errors will take the forms of omissions and substitutions (the classifica-

115

tion of "distortion" is omitted from our discussion, for distortions are nothing more than substitutions) .

1. *Dictation* (to be read by examiner)

The sun shone brightly that day, in startling contrast to the mood of those attending the conference. They had gathered together from all parts of the nation as soon as the news had broken It seemed incredible, but it was true. Fate had dealt another crushing blow, and now their leader was dead. It was their job, those gathered here, to select his successor. They were humbled by the enormity of the task. As the hand faltered, so might the flame. It was their task to select the new keeper of the flame, and in this moment of grief, despair, and fear, they sought Divine intercession and guidance. They longed for the comfort of eternity.

2. *Free-style composition* (request student to write a passage about his experiences in studying the English language.)

3. *Contextual Phonemic Discrimination* (read by the examiner; student identifies the order of the readings.)

A. 1. He sawed it.
    2. He saw it.

B. 1. She bought the best.
    2. She bought the vest.

C. 1. He thought a lot.
    2. He taught a lot.

D. 1. His speech was viewed.
    2. His speech was booed.

E. 1. Give me the vise.
    2. Give me the vase.

F. 1. She fixed the theme.
    2. She fixed the seam.

G. 1. I have to chew it.
    2. I have to shoe it.

H. 1. Look at the hall!
    2. Look at the hole!

I.   1. He slipped.
      2. He slept.
J.   1. Give me the pen!
      2. Give me the pan!

4. *Echoic Response* (each word read first by the examiner, then repeated by the student.)

Symbol	Key Word	Student's Pronunciation	
		Right	*Wrong*
/p/	*p*ig		
/b/	*b*a*b*y		
/m/	*m*an		
/θ/	*th*in		
/ð̆/	fa*th*er		
/t/	*t*oy		
/d/	*d*oo*d*le		
/n/	fu*nn*y		
/l/	fe*l*t		
/k/	pa*ck*et		
/g/	*g*o		
/f/	*f*un		
/v/	pa*v*ement		
/ng/	shini*ng*		
/s/	*s*ee		
/z/	bu*zz*ing		
/sh/	na*ti*on		
/zh/	mea*s*ure		
/tsh/	*ch*ur*ch*		
/dzh/	*j*u*dg*e		
/r/	me*rr*y		
/w/	*w*e		
/j/	*y*es		
/h₁/	*h*orse		
/h₂/	a*h*ead		
/i/	s*ea*t		
/I/	h*i*t		

Symbol	Key Word	Student's Pronunciation	
		Right	*Wrong*
/e/	s*ai*l		
/ɛ/	g*e*t		
/æ/	s*a*t		
/ɑ/	s*o*d		
/ɔ/	t*au*ght		
/o/	s*oa*p		
/U/	st*oo*d		
/u/	s*ui*t		
/uh/	bl*oo*d		
/ə/	*a*bove		
/ɝ/	b*ir*d		
/er/	fath*er*		
/aI/	*eye*		
/Iu/	b*eau*ty		
/aU/	n*ow*		
/ɔI/	r*oy*al		

5. *Reading Discrimination*

a. Isolated words — (read by student)	*Right*	*Wrong*
far		
late		
for		
put		
house		
vision		
judge		
street		
thumb		
dishes		
am		
see		
go		
bird		
hear		
chicken		
letter		

sleet
lollipop
western
get
in
rule
noise
day
birthday
barrel
think
ship
Virginia

b. Connected words — (read by student)

Types of errors

When he heard the answer he was horrified.
You've certainly met your match.
List, at least, the most important ones.
He said he was sad.
They watched the turkey shoot.

6. *Aural Comprehension* (read by examiner. Student writes only the answers to the questions that follow.)

Tom and Michael worked in the cafeteria at their university. This was their means of gaining extra spending money at school. Their job entailed clearing tables, washing dishes, and sweeping the cafeteria. Both boys disliked the job, but viewed it as a necessity.

Their favorite day was Sunday because they were free at noon. The evening meal was never offered on that day. Their Sundays were spent in studying or relaxing at the beach. They worked hard at making Sunday a day of leisure.

1. Where did the boys work?
2. What were their duties?
3. What was their favorite day?
4. Why was Sunday a free day?
5. How did they spend their Sundays?

MORAN SURVEY OF ENGLISH USAGE
(Score Sheet)

Written Section

#1. Dictation
#2. Free-style Composition

		Spelling Errors		Word Omissions		Word Order	Punctuation	
	Gross Errors	Vowel Substitutions	Consonant Substitutions	Whole Word	Part of Word	Incorrect Order	Missing	In-Correct
Dictation								
Free-Style Composition								

Contextual Phonemic Discrimination

(List number of correct responses. Possible high score 10) ——————.

Aural/Oral Response (List number of correct responses)
    a. Echoic Response   (E)   (Possible high score 43) ——————.
    b. Reading Discrimination

        1. Isolated words   (RI)   (Possible high score 30) ——————.
        2. Connected words (RC)

Vowel Substitutions		
Consonant Substitutions		
Vowel Omissions		
Consonant Omissions		

Oral Comprehension

(List number of correct responses. Possible high score 5) ——————.

INDEX OF NAMES

Akin, J., 107
Alcorn, K., 28, 103
Alcorn, S., 28, 103

Bedford, R., v
Benny, J., 30
Black, J., 17, 40, 79, 103
Block, B., 103
Boomsliter, P., v
Brigance, W., 107
Bronstein, A., 103, 104, 107, *see* Stevens
Brown, S., 109, *see* Johnson
Burk, K., 103
Burkowsky, M., 73, 103
Byrne, M., 107
Bzoch, K., v

Carr, E., 103
Carrell, J., 107
Cartier, F., 103
Chreist, F., 41
Clark, S., 108
Croft, K., 103
Curtis, J., 109

Davis, S., 104, 107
Dew, D., v
Diehl, C., 103
DiMichael, E., 109, *see* King
Downs, P., vi
Duffy, J., v

Edney, C., 109
Eisenson, J., 108

Fairbanks, G., 42, 103
Fisher, H., 108
Fulton, R., 108

Genauer, J., vi
Gleason, H., 103

Gordon, M., 108
Green, H., 104, *see* Potter, *also see* Kopp, H., 109

Hanley, T., 108
Hawk, S., 28, 105, *see* Young
Henderson, F., 107
Hibbit, G., 108
Hinely, J., 104, *see* Newmark

Irwin, R., 103
Irwin, R. B., 109
Ives, S., 103

Jacoby, B., 107
Jancosek, E., 103
Jann, Ward and Jann, 27, 103
Johnson, W., 42, 109
Judson, L., 4, 104

Keaster, J., 109
Kenyon, J., 47, 104
King, R., 109
Kopp, G., v, 104, *see* Potter
Kopp, H., 109, *see* Green
Knott, T., 104
Kriedler, C., 104, *see* Robinett

Lado, R., 104
Larudee, F., 104
Leon, P., v
Leutenegger, R., 104, *see* Pickler
Lieberman, P., 109
Lloyd, D., v, 104
Long, R., 104, *see* Robinett

MacDonald, E., 4, 104
Macleish, A., 104, *see* Robinett
MacPherson, R., 27, 104
Mayer, E., v, 18, 41, 104
Mintz, J., 104, *see* Newmark

Moran, M., v, 111, 115
Morrison, T., v
Moses, E., 104, 109

Nemoy, E., 42, 104, 107
Newmark, L., 104
Nichols, 104
Norman, R., 108, see Hibbit
Nutley, G., 104, see Robinett

Pickler, J., 104
Potter, R., 104
Prator, C., 40, 46, 104

Rambo, D., 103
Robinett, B., 104

Satz, P., 103
Schueler, H., 104
Schwartz, R., 104, see Robinett
Singh, S., 103
Smith, H., 104, 105

Stevens, C., 104
Sutherland, K., 104

Takefuta, Y., 103
Thomas, C., 109
Thurman, W., 108
Tiffany, W., 107
Tosi, O., 103
Trager, G., 103, 105
Trueblood, T., 108

Van Riper, C., 42, 110
Voxland, H., vi, 80

Warfel, H., 104
Weaver, A., 4, 104, see Judson, 104
West, R., v
White, R., 103
Wise, C., 105
Wong, H., 104, see Stevens

Young, E., 28, 105

SUBJECT INDEX

Age, 9
Arithmetic, 99
Articulation Testing, 62, 63
Articulators, 7, 22 ff.
Articulatory movements, 23, 49-54
Attention, focussing of, 17
Audiovisual, 11, 13, 14
Auditory discrimination, 18, 19, 47, 64-66
Auditory feedback, 21
Auditory memory, 66-68
Auditory training, 17-21, 23, 28
Aural comprehension, 119

Bell & Howell Language Master, 12
Blending, 4
Blind children, 28

C A E, 3-9, 19, 20, 30, 42, 43, 70, 86, 87
Categories, 31, 32, 90-95
Center for Applied Linguistics, 39
Cerebration, 26
Choral reading, 97, 98
Communication, 45
Connected Speech, 6
Communication, 45 ff.
Composition, 116
Consonant, 6, 19, 49-54
Context, use of, 30-33
Culture, 9, 24

Dating standards, 36
Deaf children, 28
Dialect, 6
Dictation, 19, 116
Diphthongs, 6, 24
Drill, 14, sources of, 38-43
Dynamics, 13

Echoic response, 117
Elocutionary texts, 41
Embarrassment, 24

Emotion, 7
Epilogue, 101

Facial movements, 16, 22
Frictional noise, 22

Grouping, 14-16, 77-80
Group therapy, 77-100

Hearing problems, 18, 24
Homesick, 36
Humor, 30, 31, 33

Idioms, 9, 31
Individual therapy, 16, 55 ff.
Initial interview, 56-57
Intensity, 7
I P A, 47

Jargon, 9

Key words, 49 ff.
Kinesthesia, 26-29
Kinesthetic-proprioceptive, 17, 26-29

Laboratory assistant, 12
Language laboratory, 12
Liaison, 5, 6, 81 ff.
Lingual movements, 16
Linking, see liaison
Lipreading, 22
Loudness differentiation, 20

Minimal pairs, 18, 19
Mirror practice, 13, 23, 24, 25, 28
Modern Language Association of America, 38
Moral standards, 36
Motivation, 18, 30-37
Mouth opening, 24

National Association for Foreign Student Affairs, 38
National Council of Teachers of English, 38
Nationalism, 15

Pedogogical media, 11 ff.
Phonation, 26, 27
Phonemes, 19, 23, 47
Phonemic difficulties, 21
Phonemic discrimination, 116
Phonetics, 22 ff., 47, 49-54, 60-66
Phrase-building, 74, 75
Phrases, pattern of, 8, 23, 42, 87-89
Pitch, 20
Pitch discrimination, 20
Pitch change, 7
Poetry, 32
Prepositions, 74, 75
Pronunciation, basic concepts, 5-9
Proprioception, 26-29

Readers Digest, 13, 59
Reading aloud, 32, 60
Reading discrimination, 118
Resonance, 26, 27, 29
Respiration, 26, 27
Rivalry, 21, 98-99 ff.
Role-playing, 98
Rules for pronunciation, 4-10, 55, 69-73, 80-82, 112

Scheduling, 47-48
Seashore tests, 20

Sensorineural hearing loss, 24
Sensory modality, 9
Speech and language games, 98-100
Soft palate, 8
Sound films, 12
Speech Association of America, 38
Speech disorders, 22
Speech mechanism, 8
Speech pattern, 6
Stress, 6, 8, 88, 89, 96, 97
Stutterers, 22
Style, 45 ff.
Substitutions, 7, 8

Tadoma approach, 28
Tape recorder, 9, 12, 20, 21
TESOL, 38 ff.
Termination of training, 101
Therapy
  individual, 55-76
  group, 77-100
  termination, 101
Timing, 7
Tongue placement, 28

Unvoicing, 23

Visual aid, 11, 12, 13
Visual training, 17, 22 ff.
Vocal cord vibration, 23
Vowels, 6 ff., 19, 24, 25, 49-54

Wives, 35